IMPERIALISM AND FREE TRADE: LANCASHIRE AND INDIA
IN THE MID-NINETEENTH CENTURY

IMPERIALISM AND FREE TRADE:

LANCASHIRE AND INDIA

IN THE

MID-NINETEENTH CENTURY

PETER HARNETTY

UNIVERSITY OF BRITISH COLUMBIA PRESS
VANCOUVER

IMPERIALISM AND FREE TRADE: LANCASHIRE AND INDIA
IN THE MID-NINETEENTH CENTURY

Library of Congress Catalogue Card Number 72-82413

International Standard Book Number 0–7748–0005–4

Printed in
Hong Kong

TABLE OF CONTENTS

LIST OF TABLES

This book has been published with the help of a grant from the Humanities Research Council of Canada, using funds provided by the Canada Council.

PREFACE

In writing this book, I have drawn upon a number of my published articles in which I have developed the theme of "the imperialism of free trade" as a conceptual tool in analyzing British policy in India in the middle of the nineteenth century. I wish to thank the editors of the University of Toronto Press and of the following journals for permission to do so: *Economic History Review, Journal of British Studies, Journal of Indian History,* the *Indian Economic and Social History Review,* and *Agricultural History.* Research for the book was carried out in England and India and I would like to thank the following for their assistance: Mr. S. C. Sutton and the staff of the India Office Library and the India Office Records in London; the staff of the Manchester Central Reference Library; the Earl of Harewood for permission to read the Canning Papers in the estate record office at Harewood House, near Leeds; the director of the National Archives of India in New Delhi; and the director of the Maharashtra State Record Office in Bombay. I would also like to thank the Canada Council for the financial assistance which made this research possible. Several of my colleagues at the University of British Columbia have commented on drafts of my chapters, and I express my appreciation to Dr. John Norris and Dr. Robert Kubicek without, of course, in any way holding them responsible for what I have written. I owe a special debt of thanks to Professor William L. Holland for his support, advice, and encouragement.

PETER HARNETTY

The University of British Columbia,
Vancouver, Canada.

1

INTRODUCTION

IN A FAMOUS SPEECH at the Crystal Palace on 24 June 1872, Disraeli denounced Liberalism for its policy of cutting the colonies adrift, of wanting to give up India, and of showing "with precise, with mathematical demonstration, that there never was a jewel in the Crown of England that was truly so costly as the possession of India." He continued: "those who advised that policy – and I believe their convictions were sincere – looked upon the Colonies of England, looked even upon the connection with India, as a burden upon this country; viewing everything in a financial aspect. . . ."[1] His comments upon mid-Victorian attitudes to empire, which were clearly intended to discredit his Liberal opponents as separatists, passed into the subsequent historiography of the period.[2] Writers of such different outlooks as Hobson, Lenin, Langer, and many others agreed that mid-Victorian "indifference" and late-Victorian "enthusiasm" were directly related to the rise and decline of free trade beliefs.[3] The

[1]George Erle Buckle, *The Life of Benjamin Disraeli, Earl of Beaconsfield* (London: John Murray, 1920), V, p. 195.

[2]For a discussion of the significance of the Crystal Palace Speech, see Stanley R. Stembridge, "Disraeli and the Millstones," *Journal of British Studies*, V (1965–66), pp. 122–39.

[3]J. A. Hobson, *Imperialism: A Study*, 3rd edition (London: G. Allen and Unwin, 1938), pp. 99–109; V. I. Lenin, "Imperialism: The Highest Stage of Capitalism," *Selected Works: Two-Volume Edition* (Moscow, 1947), I, pp. 642, 674, 686–87; W. L. Langer,

impetus behind the "Little Englandism" of the mid-Victorians was said to be the Manchester School, which favoured retrenchment, was anti-militaristic, and was coldly unsentimental in measuring the value of the empire in terms of what it cost the British taxpayer.

The charge that the Manchester School was indifferent and even hostile to empire has been repeatedly echoed by modern historians. The Danish scholar Bodelsen, whose *Studies in Mid-Victorian Imperialism* became a classic work on the subject, called the Manchester School "the centre of separatism."[4] Similarly, the Canadian historian, D. G. Creighton, argued that the first half of Queen Victoria's reign, from the coronation to the early 1870s, was the period of lack of faith in the empire, lack of belief in its value, and lack of interest in its continuance. "Under the inspired leadership of the Manchester School, the whole political and economic world of Great Britain made a determined assault upon the second empire."[5] And the American historian R. S. Schuyler identified the 1860s as the high water mark of anti-imperial feeling. "The decade 1861–70 may fairly be called a critical period in British imperial history," he wrote, "for it was in these years that tendencies in Britain towards the disruption of the Empire reached their climax."[6]

Subsequently, this long-standing interpretation was challenged by two British historians, John Gallagher and Ronald Robinson. They suggested that the mid-nineteenth century was not a period of indifference to empire; rather it was one of large-scale expansion and the successful exploitation of empire – both formal and informal – in such places as India, Latin America, and Canada. They argued that there was an essential continuity of policy in the Victorian period. In the age of so-called anti-imperialism, existing colonies were retained, new ones obtained, and new spheres of influence set up. The growth of British industry made new demands on British policy. It necessitated linking undeveloped areas with British foreign trade. In both the formal and informal dependencies in the mid-Victorian period, there was much effort to open continental interiors, expand British influence inland from the ports, and develop the hinterlands. The general strategy of this development was to convert these areas into complementary satellite economies providing raw materials and food for

The Diplomacy of Imperialism, 1890–1902, 2nd edition (New York: Alfred Knopf, 1951), p. 76. Hobson was the first to link the new imperialism of the late nineteenth century with the decline of free trade beliefs. The first edition of *Imperialism: A Study* appeared in 1902.

[4]C. A. Bodelsen, *Studies in Mid-Victorian Imperialism* (Copenhagen: Glydendal, 1924), p. 33.

[5]D. G. Creighton, "The Victorians and the Empire," *Canadian Historical Review*, XIX (1938), p. 145.

[6]R. S. Schuyler, *The Fall of the Old Colonial System* (New York: Oxford University Press, 1945), p. 245.

Great Britain and also providing widening markets for her manufactures. Far from being an era of "indifference," the mid-Victorian years were the decisive stage in the history of British expansion overseas, in that the combination of technological innovation, commercial penetration, and political influence allowed Great Britain to command those economies which could be made to fit best into her own.[7]

To illustrate their thesis, Gallagher and Robinson pointed to India which, in this period, instead of being evacuated, was subjected to intensive development along the best mercantilist lines. The characteristics of so-called imperialist expansion at the end of the nineteenth century developed in India long before the date – about 1880 – which Lenin believed the age of economic imperialism opened. Direct governmental promotion of products required by British industry, governmental manipulation of tariffs to help British exports, railway construction at high and guaranteed rates of interest to open the continental interior – all of these techniques of direct political control were employed in ways which seem alien to the so-called age of *laissez-faire*.[8]

The Gallagher and Robinson thesis has found both support and contradiction in the work of other historians. Even before they published their hypothesis in 1953, H. J. Habakkuk had pointed out that the Acts passed between 1846–49, which placed the empire on a free trade basis, did not mark any change in the assumptions of British manufacturers about the role of colonies in British economic life. After 1846 colonies, as before, were to be the source of raw materials and markets for British goods. The opinion of manufacturers in England was unable to prevail against Canada's decision to place heavy import duties on manufactures which could be produced domestically, but it was able to delay by twenty years the establishment of tariff reciprocity among the Australian colonies and it was effective in determining the tariff policy of India. Such efforts by English manufacturers to control colonial tariffs point to the persistence of certain elements of mercantilist psychology in their attitude to the colonies.[9]

On the other hand, opponents of the Gallagher and Robinson thesis have reiterated the genuine commitment of mid-nineteenth century British politicians and civil servants to *laissez-faire* doctrines and their reluctance to allow themselves to become politically involved anywhere in the world. It was the change in this outlook after 1880 that constituted a revolution in British imperial policy and ushered in the "new imperialism" of the

[7]John Gallagher and Ronald Robinson, "The Imperialism of Free Trade," *Economic History Review,* 2nd ser., VI (1953), pp. 1–15.

[8]Ibid., p. 4.

[9]H. J. Habakkuk, "Free Trade and Commercial Expansion, 1853–1870," *Cambridge History of the British Empire,* II (1940), p. 753.

last decade of the nineteenth century. With some force, critics have rejected the notion of an "invisible empire of informal sway" whereby Great Britain was able to secure her principal economic objectives in the backward economies by means short of formal annexation.[10] With much less force, they have argued that the concept of "the imperialism of free trade" is a misnomer even when applied to India as part of the formal empire. One such critic has stated:

> It is perfectly true that the Manchester School approved and supported public investment and guarantees in India, but Britain was already committed in India. Whatever theoretical objections Cobden and Bright might have had to imperial expansion, they were aware that withdrawal from India could end in anarchy and chaos. Determined as they were to avoid any similar imperial commitment in the future, for the present they could see no genuine alternative to encouraging the development of India with a view to the progress of trade and, perhaps eventually, to some measure of self-government.[11]

There are two main objections to this argument. First, India was not just an inherited empire in the mid-nineteenth century. Expansion continued after the victory of free trade in 1846: the Punjab was annexed in 1849, Berar and Nagpur in 1853, and Oudh in 1856, to mention only the largest acquisitions. And Berar and Nagpur were annexed specifically with an eye to their cotton-producing potential.[12] Second, it is historically impossible to consider mid-Victorian attitudes to empire while excluding from consideration the most important part of the empire, India.[13]

[10] W. M. Mathew, "The Imperialism of Free Trade: Peru, 1820–70," *Econ. Hist. Rev.*, 2nd ser., XXI (1968), pp. 562–79. This is one of the few attempts that have been made to test, by means of a case study, the validity of the Gallagher and Robinson thesis of an informal empire in underlying unity with the formal empire and subject to the same political influences designed to further the commercial interests of the imperial power. Generally, historians who reject the Gallagher and Robinson thesis do so on the ground that whether an area was formally or informally controlled is a fundamental distinction. If it was formally a British possession, they argue, all kinds of other factors come into play to overlay, twist, and modify economic and commercial pressures: the Anti-Slavery Act, judicial procedures, the ambitions of career officials, pressures by British subjects domiciled in the colony or protectorate, and simply the sheer problems of ruling vast areas with skeletal staffs and little money.

[11] D. C. M. Platt, "The Imperialism of Free Trade: Some Reservations," *Econ. His. Rev.*, 2nd ser., XXI (1968), p. 296, n. 3. The danger of making exceptions in studying the formal empire lies in deciding where to draw the line. If India was an exceptional case, then so was Ireland. Every colony was in some degree "exceptional."

[12] "Especially I wish to draw to your attention the bearing wh. the occupation of Nagpore and previously of Berar have upon your manufacturing difficulty, the supply of raw cotton." Dalhousie to Wood, 4 March 1854. Halifax Collection (India Office Library, MSS. Eur. F. 78), India Board, Correspondence, India, bundle 18.

[13] On the neglect of India by writers on imperial history, see Holden Furber, "The Theme of Imperialism and Colonialism in Modern Historical Writing on India," C. H. Philips (ed.), *Historians of India, Pakistan and Ceylon* (London: Oxford University Press, 1961), pp. 332–43.

Moreover, with the replacement of the East India Company by Crown rule in 1858 – a change long demanded by Lancashire – India was more closely integrated into the empire than ever before. The Secretary of State for India now exercised detailed control over the Indian administration. At the same time, as the minister solely responsible for Indian affairs, he was far more susceptible to political pressure groups, such as the Lancashire cotton lobby, than his predecessor, the President of the Board of Control, had been; for the latter had shared his responsibilities with the Company's Court of Directors.

It is therefore historically valid to examine mid-Victorian attitudes to empire in terms of Indian policy. Such an examination is fruitful for a number of reasons. First, it demonstrates the fallaciousness of the charge that the Manchester School looked upon the connection with India as a burden and was unaware of the importance of India to British trade. In the second place, it reveals the continuity of British imperial policy in the nineteenth century, notably in the effort to develop backward areas to suit the needs of British industry.[14] This is important because most of the economic explanations of the "new imperialism" of the late nineteenth century depend on the assumption that it can be linked with the particular stage of development reached by capital and industry at that time.[15] Lastly, it indicates, as other scholars have argued, that in the mid-nineteenth century one can discern clear manifestations of that spirit which may properly be denominated "economic imperialism."[16]

For the purposes of this analysis, "economic imperialism" is seen as simply one aspect of the wider phenomenon termed "imperialism." It reflects an attitude of mind to the possession and use of dependent territories by the metropolitan power.[17] As one historian has put it: "if imperialism is the dominion of one group over another, economic imperialism is the establishment or exploitation of such dominion for continuing material advantage."[18] Imperialism clearly involves subordination; the

[14]David Fieldhouse has argued for continuity in British imperial policy going back into the eighteenth century. See his chapter "British Imperialism in the Late Eighteenth Century: Defence or Opulence?" in Kenneth Robinson and Frederick Madden (eds.), *Essays in Imperial Government Presented to Margery Perham* (Oxford: Basil Blackwell, 1963).

[15]M. E. Chamberlain, *The New Imperialism* (London: Historical Association, 1970), p. 19.

[16]Leland H. Jenks, *The Migration of British Capital to 1875* (New York: Alfred Knopf, 1927), pp. 195–97.

[17]Fieldhouse, op. cit., p. 23.

[18]David S. Landes, "Some Thoughts on the Nature of Economic Imperialism," *Journal of Economic History*, XXI (1961), p. 496. And A. P. Thornton has remarked that "The entire English connection with India, with all that had sprung from it, was the direct product of commercial imperialism." *Doctrines of Imperialism* (New York: Wiley, 1965), p. 108. Chapter III of Thornton's book is an extended discussion of "The Doctrine of Profit" as an element in imperialism.

indicative phenomena of economic imperialism are those episodes in which the arts of political manipulation gave aid to the craft of enterprise and in which the dominion employed by the superior power is associated with wilful and effective subordination.[19] This book is concerned with the ways in which British dominion over India in the middle decades of the nineteenth century was exercised in the interests of the Lancashire cotton industry. It shows the persistence among Lancashire cotton manufacturers of a mercantilist attitude towards the Indian empire. This attitude was tersely stated in 1862 by Thomas Bazley, president of the Manchester Chamber of Commerce from 1845–59 and member of Parliament for Manchester from 1858–80: "The great interest of India was to be agricultural rather than manufacturing and mechanical."[20] But this mercantilist view expressed itself in policy demands which show the imperialism inherent in free trade attitudes to empire in the middle of the nineteenth century. The full development of India as a source of agricultural raw materials (and this meant, of course, cotton) was inhibited by the Indian cotton duties which, by protecting native manufactures, caused the consumption in India of large quantities of raw cotton that otherwise, i.e., under "free competition," would be exported to Great Britain.[21] It followed that the duties must be abolished, thereby both enhancing the supply of cotton for British industry and enlarging the market in India for British manufactured goods. Such a policy could be justified on theoretical grounds by the doctrines of free trade. But to encourage India as a producer of raw materials required more than economic freedom. It also involved a contradictory policy of governmental paternalism. Lancashire demanded that the Government of India inspire the development of private enterprise in the Indian empire by financing some of this development. In line with this demand, the authorities in India guaranteed railway construction and undertook numerous public works. They also undertook the experimental cultivation of cotton and, in this connection, made the first attempt at state interference in India in the fields of production, marketing, and trade.

In all these measures, India's effective subordination to British imperial power was clearly revealed. And all these policies were undertaken at the behest of free traders at a time when *laissez-faire* attitudes supposedly generated indifference, if not hostility, to empire. An examination of each of these policies in the chapters that follow illustrates the relevance of the concept of "the imperialism of free trade" in explaining mid-nineteenth century British policy in India.

[19]Cf. Mathew, "The Imperialism of Free Trade: Peru, 1820–70," op. cit., p. 563.
[20]*Cotton Supply Reporter*, February 1862.
[21]Petition from the Mayor, Aldermen, and Burgesses of Burnley, Lancs., to the Secretary of State, 6 Aug. 1862. India Office, Revenue Dept., Home Corresp., Letters Rec., IV, no. 353.

2

THE INDIAN COTTON DUTIES, *1859-82*

"I CANNOT DENY THAT ENGLAND . . . may, with some reason, ask India so to levy the necessary Revenue as not to interfere injuriously with trade between the two countries," said the Indian Finance Member, Samuel Laing, in the Legislative Council on 17 April 1862. He was expressing an attitude to India which British cotton manufacturers had held since the abolition of the East India Company's commercial monopoly in 1813 and which they sustained throughout the nineteenth century. They consistently viewed India as a vast market for their products and they were determined to capture and exploit it to the greatest extent possible. Thus, in 1814 they secured a system of tariff duties which allowed British manufactures to enter India at a nominal rate, permitted raw cotton to leave India at a nominal duty, but retained the high British tariffs which put Indian cotton manufactures at a considerable disadvantage in the British market. Throughout the period from 1814 to 1859, British exports to India were able to enter the country at low rates: in the case of cotton, 5 per cent on piece goods and $3\frac{1}{2}$ per cent on yarn. Yet the Indian finances were in a chaotic state. During the same forty-five year period, the Government of India incurred deficits in thirty-three years, so that, to quote another Indian Finance Member, James Wilson, "the normal state of Indian finances may be said to be deficiency of income and addition

7

to debt."[1] Yet efforts to increase income were limited mainly to raising the tax on land, with consequent burdens on the peasants. The interests of British manufacturers ruled out any increase in the tariff.

By 1857 the Government of India was beginning to protest against this situation. Early in the year, the Governor-General, Lord Canning, warned the Home authorities that he anticipated a "very ugly deficit for 1856–57" to meet which new sources of revenue would have to be found, and he proposed an increase in the import duties.[2] Canning's proposal had the strong and unanimous support of the Governor-General's Council, although they knew that it would provoke opposition from Lancashire. A member of the Council, J. P. Grant, cogently expressed the Government of India's case for import duties in a statement which represented the substance of the Indian position in the ensuing quarter century of conflict with Lancashire.

Grant maintained that the interests of India demanded that the customs duties should provide a substantial part of the revenues just as they did in independent maritime countries. Provided that the rate of duty did not check consumption, an import duty was the least objectionable and most convenient tax that could be imposed. In India, the existing rates of duty were far below the level that would check consumption, and revenue derived from import duties provided only one-twentieth of the total revenue, compared with one-third in Great Britain. India retained many other more vexatious taxes, not in the best interests of those who paid them, but in the imaginary interests of the dominant country. Grant said:

> I say imaginary because I am convinced that what is best for India is, ultimately, best also for Manchester. It was but a part of the very same policy which has prescribed to India differential duties, to the unjust discouragement of her trade with all the world, except Great Britain and her possessions. It is impossible to attribute any regard for the interests of Indian consumers the general lowness of the rates of a tariff, when by that tariff those consumers are prevented by double duties from buying what they want in the cheapest market.[3]

[1]Financial statement by James Wilson, Finance Member, Governor-General's Council 18 Feb. 1860. India, *Legislative Council Proceedings*, vol. 6 (1860), p. 100. Dalhousie fought a war against the Sikhs in 1848–49 and another in Burma in 1852. The administrative expenses of government rose considerably as a result of his extensive territorial acquisitions, including Nagpur, which he wanted as a great cotton-producing area. When Canning became Governor-General in 1856 he found himself involved in a war with Persia.

[2]Canning to W. H. Sykes, Chairman, East India Company, 8 March 1857. Canning Papers (Leeds Public Library, England), 31 (Letters to the Court of Directors), no. 26.

[3]Minute by the Hon. J. P. Grant, 20 Jan. 1857. India, Collections to Despatches (Separate Revenue), III (1859), no. 4.

Grant appealed for the elimination of differential duties, whereby foreign goods entered India at a higher rate than British goods; the abolition of the tax on trades and professions in Madras presidency; reduction of the salt tax in Bengal; and a moderate increase in the import duties.

In sum, Grant was asking for a tariff policy geared to Indian interests and not to those of British manufacturers. This was to be a recurring theme over the next twenty-five years in the Government of India's resistance to pressure from London for a tariff policy acceptable to the Lancashire cotton interests.

The outbreak of the Indian Rebellion in May 1857 postponed action on Canning's proposal for an increase in the import duties. But the heavy expenditures incurred by the Government of India in suppressing the revolt made the question more urgent. Early in 1859 Canning warned Lord Stanley, who had become the first Secretary of State for India the previous September, that the financial prospects for 1859–60 were not cheering. Recourse must be had to new or increased taxes, and they must be put into operation as quickly as possible. Apart from the ordinary expenses of government in India, an additional strain on the finances arose from railway works amounting to £4 million. Two possibilities immediately available were an increase in the tariff and an extension of the stamp duties. Canning said he had long ago expressed the opinion that import duties should be raised and the Court of Directors had more than once said that the whole matter was under consideration. Now there was no longer time to ask for instructions. The Government of India intended to raise the customs duties, and trusted that the British Government would support this step. "Of course, there will be an outcry from Manchester;" wrote Canning, "but with such pressing necessity staring us in the face, and the fact that the Tariff will remain a moderate one – so moderate that I look confidently to an almost undiminished consumption – I hope our case will be thought a good one."[4]

Canning wasted little time, although there was greater diversity of rates and systems in the different presidencies than he supposed, and this delayed the formulation of the new policy until 4 March 1859.[5] The Government proposed to improve its financial situation by raising the import duties through the abolition of differential duties and by the imposition of a general rate of 20 per cent on imported luxury goods and 10 per cent on other goods, except for cotton twist on which the rate would be 5 per cent. There was also to be a small increase in the export duty on grain, but

[4]Canning to Stanley, 8 Feb. 1859. Canning Papers 36 (Letters to the Secretary of State, 1858–59), no. 154.
[5]Enclosed in Government of India to Secretary of State, Letter no. 6 (Separate Revenue), 14 Mar. 1859. Collections to Despatches (Sep. Rev.), III, no. 13. The Resolution was published in the *Calcutta Gazette* on 14 March.

the export duties on raw silk and tobacco were to be repealed. This was the basis of the Customs Duties Bill introduced into the Legislative Council on 12 March 1859, and passed by it two days later. In speaking on the Bill, Canning stressed the urgency of the financial situation, in particular the budgetary deficit of 817 lakhs for the year 1857–58; the deficit of more than 1,300 lakhs which was expected for 1858–59; and the interest charges on two large loans that the Government had raised to tide it over its difficulties – one of £8 million in Great Britain and another of 914 lakhs in India. Anticipating reactions from Manchester, Canning admitted that the increased duty on cotton piece goods from 5 to 10 per cent was considerable, but pointed out that the trade in piece goods had taken a deep root in India and currently exceeded £3 million a year in value. The trade in cotton twist was not so well established; being a partly manufactured article it tended to promote Indian industry. Canning therefore argued that a lower rate of 5 per cent was justifiable.[6]

For the moment, the critical state of the Indian finances over-rode dogmatic free trade arguments and arguments of imperial interest. The British Government, the British mercantile community in India, and Lancashire were all prepared to accept, with varying degrees of warmth, the necessity of raising the import duties. Stanley assured Canning of the full support of the British Government in a letter written on 18 March 1859. He said that he would have preferred consultation on the subject before action was taken and added that he had been working on a scheme for a new tariff with the finance committee of his Council. There was now no need for him to go on with it, and he told the Governor-General that "there can be no doubt you are right in acting without delay, in an exigency like the present."[7] Stanley declared that there was no need to fear an outcry from Manchester; if there was one he could deal with it, but the necessity of India's case was well understood in Britain. Formal approval was transmitted to India soon after in a despatch in which the British Government endorsed the equalization of duties on British and foreign manufactures and supported the proposal to achieve the equalization not by a reduction of the duties on foreign goods to the British level but by an increase in the rate of duty on British goods to the foreign level. It also

---

[6]India, *Legislative Council Proceedings*. vol. 5 (1859), p. 118. The Customs Duties Bill became law as Act VII of 1859. (A lakh of rupees (Rs. 100,000) was equivalent to £10,000 at this time. Hence the deficits mentioned by Canning amounted to £8,170,000 and £13,000,000 respectively. In fact, the actual deficits for 1857–58 and 1858–59 came to £8,390,000 and £14,187,000 respectively. See Sir Charles Wood's statement in the House of Commons on 17 July 1862. Great Britain, *Parliamentary Debates*, 3rd series, vol. CLXVIII, col. 449.)

[7]Stanley to Canning, 18 Mar. 1859. Canning Papers, 6 (Letters from the Secretary of State, 1858–59), no. 100. Stanley repeated this assurance in the House of Commons on 15 Apr. 1859. *Parl. Deb.*, 3rd ser., CLIII, col. 1811.

accepted the reasons for lower duties on cotton twist given by Canning in his speech to the Legislative Council. The British Government reluctantly consented to the retention of export duties because of the financial crisis, but expressed its opposition to them in principle. Regarding the increased import duties, the British Government agreed that the rates of duty levied in India were on the whole very moderate and it sanctioned the higher rates. In fact it was prepared to accept a rate of $7\frac{1}{2}$ per cent on cotton twist and yarn, which was $2\frac{1}{2}$ per cent above that actually adopted by the Government of India.[8]

From the British mercantile community in India, little opposition was encountered. Public meetings in Madras and Bombay protested not so much against the higher rates, as the haste with which they had been imposed.[9] British merchants in India claimed that the sudden imposition of the new rates entailed heavy losses for importers who had contracted to deliver goods at a fixed price which included duty.[10] Their opposition was checked when they realized that under the Act imposing the higher duties, contractors were authorized to increase the price of such goods by an amount equal to the difference between the new duty and the old.

In Lancashire, the Liverpool East India and China Association wrote to the Secretary of State expressing itself as "deeply sensible of the difficulties in which the Indian government was placed," which warranted the increase in import duties. The Association hoped that they would be removed as soon as possible.[11] In Manchester the reaction was less sympathetic. The directors of the Chamber of Commerce passed a resolution of protest against the duties and called the Government of India's policy in raising them "highly impolitic" and injurious to the trading interests of both countries as well as a serious interference with commercial freedom.[12] Nothing further was done at the time, however, and the matter was not raised in Parliament. The reason undoubtedly was the gravity of the financial situation in India which muted even Lancashire objections to higher tariffs. Nevertheless, Manchester let its views be known to James Wilson, who resigned as Vice-President of the Board of Trade in 1859 to go to India as Finance Member of the Governor-General's

[8]Secretary of State to Government of India, Despatch no. 4 (Sep. Rev.), 7 Apr. 1859.

[9]India Office, Revenue Dept., Home Correspondence, Letters Received, I, no. 28 for resolutions passed by a public meeting in Madras on 25 Mar. 1859; Collections to Despatches (Sep. Rev.), III, no. 13 for a telegram from Government of Bombay to Government of India, 16 Mar. 1859 containing a memorial adopted by a meeting of the Bombay mercantile community on 15 Mar. 1859.

[10]Memorial from the Bombay Chamber of Commerce to the Governor of Bombay, 15 Mar. 1859.

[11]Peter Ewart, Chairman of the East India and China Association, to Secretary of State, 31 May 1859. I. O., Rev. Dept., Home Corresp. Letters Rec., I, no. 38.

[12]*Proceedings of the Manchester Chamber of Commerce* (Manchester Central Reference Library), vol. 6 (1858–67), 12 May 1859.

Council. The directors of the Manchester Chamber of Commerce arranged an interview with Wilson before his departure for India and presented him with three resolutions, calling for economies in public expenditure; the raising of additional revenue by means of an income tax and a property tax rather than by increased import duties; and the encouragement of such public works as promoted the progress and prosperity of commerce and agriculture, such as railways, canals, and irrigation works.[13]

When Wilson arrived in India he came to the conclusion that changes were needed in the tariff. In the first place he considered that the 20 per cent rate on luxury articles was too high, because revenue derived from that source had drastically declined since the imposition of the higher rates. Secondly, he was surprised by the fact that although the same duties on imports applied all over India, the valuations on which *ad valorem* duties were levied varied at every port. Hence the real rate of duty varied in different parts of the country. The Government of Bengal fixed the rate for Calcutta, the Government of Bombay another rate for that presidency, and the Government of Madras still another. The Government of India, which imposed the duties, had no connection with the valuations fixed by the subordinate governments. In Calcutta the valuations were so absurdly low that Wilson calculated the Government had been losing £200,000 a year by them.[14] These valuations were fixed by a compromise between rates proposed by the Collector of Customs in Calcutta and others proposed by the Bengal Chamber of Commerce. The consequence was that those articles of trade in which the more influential merchants were principally concerned were generally much undervalued by the tariff committee of the Bengal Chamber of Commerce, which paid little attention to the valuation on commodities dealt in by small traders. The Bengal Board of Revenue confessed that the knowledge of the customs appraisers was imperfect and vague. The Head Appraiser could give no intelligible account of the way in which he arrived at his high valuation of some articles.[15]

Wilson decided to make changes, and announced them in his financial statement to the Legislative Council on 18 February 1860. He mentioned the falling off in revenue attributable to the 20 per cent rate on certain articles and announced that this rate would be reduced to 10 per cent, except in the case of tobacco. At the same time he raised the import duty on cotton twist and yarn to 10 per cent. In explaining this decision,

13Ibid., 5 Oct. 1859.

14Wilson to Wood, 15 Feb. 1860. Halifax Collection, India Office, Correspondence, India. Wood had succeeded Stanley as Secretary of State in June 1859.

15Bengal Board of Revenue to Government of Bengal, no. 265, 10 Mar. 1860. Encl. in Government of India to Secretary of State, Letter no. 16 (Sep. Rev.), 29 June 1860. Collections to Despatches (Sep. Rev.), IV, no. 29.

Wilson said he did not accept the argument that yarn should pay a lower duty because it was in an earlier stage of manufacture. He pointed out that the same could be said of grey cloth, as compared with bleached, dyed, and printed cloth. Nor did Wilson attach much importance to the argument that a low duty on yarn and a higher one on cloth encouraged native weaving. It could equally be argued that a low duty on yarn meant increased competition for the hand spinner. In this connection Wilson noted that imports of both cloth and yarn into India had risen substantially between 1857 and 1859, as shown by Table 2.1. The effect of Wilson's changes was to place a uniform tariff of 10 per cent *ad valorem* on all articles imported into India, except for beer, wine, spirits, and tobacco, to which specific duties were attached. Wilson also told the Legislative Council that the valuations upon which the *ad valorem* duties had hitherto been paid were notoriously low and were being revised.

Table 2.1
Imports of Piece Goods and Yarn into India, 1857–59

Year	Piece Goods (£)	Yarn (£)
1857	5,147,000	994,000
1858	8,497,000	1,763,000
1859	11,041,000	2,306,000

SOURCE: India, *Legislative Council Proceedings*, vol. 6 (1860), p. 120.

This would increase the revenue yield from the tariff by at least £150,000 a year. Moreover, the revised valuations would apply uniformly all over India.

The change in the table of valuations was initiated by the Bengal Board of Revenue, which drew up a new table in consultation with the Collector of Customs at Calcutta and the Bengal Chamber of Commerce, based strictly on actual prices during the past three years. The Government of India then sent the revised valuations to the Governments of Madras and Bombay. It stated that it was aware that

> nominally and professedly the duties have hitherto been intended to be the same everywhere, and that the Legislative Council has enacted the same tariff of duties; but inasmuch as they are mostly *ad valorem* duties, it must be plain that in order to secure uniformity it is essential that the valuations as well as the rates of duty shall be the same everywhere.[16]

[16]Government of India to Governments of Madras and Bombay, nos. 735–36, 7 Apr. 1860. Collections to Despatches (Sep. Rev.), IV, no. 29. An example of local

The Madras government expressed its willingness to accept the Calcutta tariff valuations with a few modifications. The Bombay government also expressed a general willingness to assimilate its tariff with that of Calcutta, although it claimed that in some respects its tariff was superior. The mercantile interests, however, were dissatisfied. In Bengal, the Calcutta commercial community objected to many of the valuations in the new tariff while in England complaints came from the Manchester Chamber of Commerce and other groups in Lancashire.

Complaints from Manchester had begun as soon as it was known that the new tariff had been approved by the Legislative Council.[17] On 19 March 1860 the directors of the Manchester Chamber of Commerce passed a resolution protesting the increase in import duties as "impolitic and unsound in principle" and requesting the British Government to withhold its sanction from any measure increasing the existing scale of duties in India. Copies of the resolution were sent to Thomas Bazley, M.P. for Manchester, and to the Secretary of State, Sir Charles Wood, with a request for an interview so that a full explanation of the opinion of the merchants of the Manchester district engaged in the India trade could be placed before him.[18] Soon after, the East India and China Association wrote to Wood expressing the "anxious hope" that he would intervene to prohibit what it called an "obnoxious tax." In particular, the Association objected that the increased duty on imported yarn, by raising its price to the Indian consumer, would give a "false and impolitic stimulus to yarn spun in India, thereby serving to keep alive the ultimately unsuccessful contest of manual power against steam machinery."[19]

Wood prepared to dig in his heels. He arranged to meet a deputation on 27 March and wrote cheerfully to Wilson: "I shall repulse my cotton twist friends tomorrow and your speech has come most opportunely to arm me with reasons."[20] The deputation consisted of six directors of the Manchester Chamber of Commerce and six members of Parliament, four of them from Lancashire.[21] It expressed its strong objections to the cotton duties for two reasons: they were "vicious in principle" and erroneous in the method by which they were to be levied. In this connection it

variations was that in Bombay duties were frequently levied on piece goods by weight, while in Calcutta they were charged by the yard or number of pieces.

[17]The Bill passed third reading on 3 Mar. 1860. The Legislative Council was notified of the Governor-General's assent to it, as Act X of 1860, on 24 Mar. 1860.

[18]*Proceedings of the Manchester Chamber of Commerce*, 19 Mar. 1860.

[19]East India and China Association to Secretary of State, 28 Mar. 1860. I. O., Rev. Dept., Home Corresp., Letters Rec., II, no. 86.

[20]Wood to Wilson, 26 Mar. 1860. Halifax Collection, India Office, Letter Books, II, p. 258.

[21]The six members of Parliament were Thomas Bazley and J. A. Turner (Manchester); J. Kershaw and J. B. Smith (Stockport); R. Dalgleish (Glasgow); and H. E. Crum Ewing (Paisley).

claimed that the duty on piece goods would in fact be about 19 per cent on their value instead of 10 per cent, while that on yarns would amount to as much as 180 per cent more than the duties previously charged. The deputation contended that this was in fact a protective duty in favour of the Indian spinner, and it asked Wood to instruct the Government of India to revise the duties. It also expressed its preference for the method of rating goods used at Bombay. The Secretary of State referred in reply to the financial difficulties of India and said he could not promise any reduction in the 10 per cent duty. He asked for detailed statements of the claim that the duties were in fact heavier than intended.[22] These were sent to Wood a week later, accompanied by samples of cloth and yarn.[23] In a written reply early in the following month, Wood repeated that he could not hold out any hope that the duty would be reduced below 10 per cent *ad valorem*. But he promised to send the correspondence to the Government of India with instructions to adjust the tariff valuations so that the duty would be levied as fairly and as equally as possible.[24]

Despite this promise, Lancashire kept up the pressure. On 22 May 1860 a special general meeting of the Manchester Chamber of Commerce was held which resolved that renewed efforts should be made to impress on the British Government and on the Government of India the injurious effects which the new import duties would have. It also decided to present a petition to the House of Commons. The burden of the petition consisted rather of a protest against the new tariff valuations than a plea for the abolition of the duties, although a reduction of the rates to 5 per cent for piece goods and $3\frac{1}{2}$ per cent for yarns was called for. The petition added that India exported more than she imported, with a consequent drain of bullion from Great Britain and Europe to meet the balance. It claimed that the new tariff would increase this drain and would harm not only the manufacturers of Great Britain but also the population of India "by diverting their industry from agricultural pursuits into much less productive channels, under the stimulus of a false system of protection."[25]

Two weeks later the directors of the Manchester Chamber of Commerce, in cooperation with a deputation from the Association of Bleachers and

[22]*Proceedings of the Manchester Chamber of Commerce*, 2 Apr. 1860; Wood to Wilson, 3 Apr. 1860. Halifax Collection, I.O., Letter Books, II, p. 262.

[23]Manchester Chamber of Commerce to Secretary of State, 7 Apr. 1860. I. O., Rev. Dept., Home Corresp., Letters Rec., II, no. 89.

[24]Assistant Under-Secretary of State to East India and China Association, and to Manchester Chamber of Commerce, 11 May 1860. I.O., Rev. Dept., Home Corresp., Letters Sent, I (1859–62, Original Drafts), nos. 14 and 15. The relevant correspondence was sent to India in Secretary of State to Government of India, Despatch no. 9 (Sep. Rev.), 17 May 1860.

[25]*Proceedings of the Manchester Chamber of Commerce*, 22 May 1860. The Petition claimed that the new valuations on piece goods and yarns meant a material addition to the duty and cited various examples to support this claim.

Dyers of Lancashire and Cheshire, resolved to send a deputation to Lord Palmerston.[26] The directors sought an interview with the Prime Minister instead of with Wood because they believed that when they had seen the Secretary of State at the end of March they had failed to impress him with the importance of the subject. At the meeting with the Prime Minister on 12 June, the deputation told Palmerston that their protest was at the mode of assessing the duties and their excessive rate. Both the Prime Minister and Wood, who was also present at the meeting, expressed their surprise at the arguments connected with the mode of assessment, and Wood promised to pass on the substance of these arguments to the Government of India.[27] The Association of Bleachers and Dyers also laid their case before the Board of Trade in the form of a memorial presented by a deputation led by James Hardcastle of Bolton. They complained of the unequal and prejudicial incidence of the revised Indian tariff in respect to unbleached and bleached goods. They argued that the difference in the value estimated for white, or bleached, goods and for grey, or unbleached, goods far exceeded the extra cost involved in the bleaching process, which was small. As a result, the duty on white goods was disproportionately high compared to the duty on grey goods. The deputation therefore asked that the duties should be levied on an *ad valorem* basis. The Board of Trade lent strong support to the bleachers' case, and asked the India Office to see that "in providing for a temporary emergency, a permanent injury be not inflicted on an important branch of the manufactures of these countries [*sic*]."[28] In the same month – June 1860 – a petition was sent to the Secretary of State signed by merchants, cotton spinners, and manufacturers of Blackburn. They claimed to represent 33,000 persons employed in spinning, weaving, and finishing cotton goods in that Lancashire town, and protested that the valuations of cotton goods on which duties were levied in India were unduly high. They requested that measures be taken for levying a uniform and fixed rate of duty not exceeding 5 per cent on the invoice price of piece goods and yarns.[29]

All this pressure began to tell on Wood. At the end of June he wrote to Wilson informing him that he had twice seen deputations of bleachers, who had complained that the new Indian tariff added upwards of a shilling to the value of bleached goods although it only cost 3d to bleach them.

[26]Ibid., 6 June 1860.

[27]Ibid., 18 June 1860.

[28]Board of Trade to Secretary of State, 25 June 1860. I. O., Rev. Dept., Home Corresp., Letters Rec., II, no. 103.

[29]Mayor of Blackburn to Secretary of State, n.d. I. O., Rev. Dept., Home Corresp., Letters Rec., II, no. 99. The reply sent by the Secretary of State on 29 June 1860 repeated what had been said in the letters to the East India and China Association and the Manchester Chamber of Commerce on 11 May 1860.

Wood asked Wilson to look into the matter, adding that he had refused all reductions of the 10 per cent *ad valorem* duty, but had promised that it would be levied as fairly as possible.[30] Wood's letter crossed one from Wilson in which the Finance Member took issue with Manchester's arguments that the new duties and valuations were hurting trade. Wilson maintained that the cotton trade was dull in India partly because stocks had accumulated up-country, and particularly because of cholera outbreaks, which in many districts had been bad enough to close fairs and markets and thus interfere with trade. He predicted that trade would revive in the cold season, and told Wood that the Government of India had decided to appoint a committee to consider the whole question of a uniform tariff.[31]

In England Wood still had to fend off attacks from Manchester. On 14 August during debate in Parliament on a motion authorizing the Secretary of State to raise a loan on behalf of the Government of India, Thomas Bazley repeated charges that the Indian tariff was injuring British trade. He claimed there was in practice a protection of 25 per cent in favour of Indian-produced goods, and that consequently mills were being rapidly constructed for manufacturing purposes in India. Wood denied these allegations and emphasized that the Indian tariff existed solely for revenue purposes. He alleged that the increase of manufacturing in India was chiefly due to British investment. He rejected a proposal made by Bazley for a countervailing excise duty on Indian manufactures, slyly adding that this was a proposition which he hardly expected from a free trader.[32]

This attitude incensed the Manchester Chamber of Commerce, which decided to draw up another memorial on the working of the Indian tariff. This document, which was sent to Wood with copies to Palmerston and Gladstone, expressed great dissatisfaction with the way in which Britain's commercial relations with India were still being treated, especially the high rate of import duties. It took exception to Wood's statement in Parliament that cotton mills recently established or projected in India were financed by British capital, but added that even if this were the case

[30]Wood to Wilson, 27 June 1860. Halifax Collection, I. O., Letter Books, III, p. 202. The memorial from the Association of Bleaching and Dyeing Trades was sent to India in Secretary of State to Government of India, Despatch no. 14 (Sep. Rev.), 18 July 1860.

[31]Wilson to Wood, 29 June 1860. Halifax Collection, I. O., Corresp., India. The committee was appointed on 29 Sept. 1860 and consisted of Richard Spooner, Commissioner of Customs, Bombay; J. N. Bullen, President, Bengal Chamber of Commerce; and Ashley Eden, Junior Secretary, Bengal Board of Revenue.

[32]*Parl. Deb.*, 3rd ser., CLX, cols. 1256–57, 14 Aug. 1860. Three cotton mills were in operation in Bombay before the increase in the import duties. Five more were built in 1860 and another three in 1861. "Statement on Cotton Spinning and Weaving Mills in Bombay Presidency," dated November 1861. Canning Papers. Miscellaneous Private Papers.

it was so because the heavy import duties would cause a reduction in Indo-British trade and so attract capital currently employed in it to such investments. The memorial also drew attention to the progress made by Great Britain in wealth and influence since the adoption of free trade as proof of the fatuity of pursuing a totally different policy in India.[33]

One reason for Manchester's sustained pressure was the death of James Wilson on 11 August 1860. As Wood remarked to Canning, Wilson's "known free trade opinions kept sober people quiet and steady; and his acknowledged ability imposed on grumblers here."[34] In October 1860 a number of directors of the Manchester Chamber of Commerce went to Glasgow for a conference with the local Chamber of Commerce, and also with Sir John Lawrence (then a member of the Secretary of State's Council) and other persons interested in the subject of trade with India. At the end of the month, the Manchester Chamber of Commerce secured an interview with the newly-appointed Finance Member, Samuel Laing.[35] In November a subcommittee on Indian import duties of the Manchester Chamber of Commerce adopted two resolutions on the subject of the duties. The first declared that these duties should be simply *ad valorem* on value at the port of entry. The second protested against the rate of duty as creating protection for Indian spinning and manufacturing, as an oppressive tax on the consumption of the masses, as inoperative for a permanently increased revenue, and as pernicious and inconsistent on the part of a nation pledged to the maintenance of free trade principles.[36]

Meanwhile the Tariff Committee had begun its labours in Calcutta, urged on by a despatch from the India Office which expressed the hope that it would produce a table of valuations which would be fair and satisfactory to all the parties interested. The despatch also expressed the view of the Secretary of State that since such a tariff would require periodic revisions to accommodate it to price fluctuations in different parts of India, these revisions should continue to be made by the local governments in consultation with the mercantile community in each presidency.[37] The Tariff Committee, whose moving spirit was Richard Spooner, the Commissioner

[33]*Proceedings of the Manchester Chamber of Commerce,* 20 Aug. 1860. Originally the memorial was to have been sent only to Palmerston, but an amendment moved by Bazley to send it to Wood also was carried by the chairman's deciding vote. The memorial was sent to Wood on 24 August.

[34]Wood to Canning, 16 Sept. 1860. Halifax Collection, I. O., Letter Books, IV, p. 152.

[35]*Proceedings of the Manchester Chamber of Commerce,* 25 Oct. and 5 Nov. 1860. The interview took place on 31 October. The Manchester deputation confined itself to two points: the mischief of specific duties on manufactured goods and the injurious effect of the 10 per cent duty on imports. Laing apparently admitted the force of the objections, and held out some hope that he would do what he could to meet them.

[36]Ibid., 16 Nov. 1860. The resolutions were sent to the India Office in December.

[37]Secretary of State to Government of India, Despatch no. 29 (Sep. Rev.), 20 Sept. 1860.

of Customs at Bombay, brought out its report on 29 October 1860.[38] The committee had been charged to consider complaints addressed to the Secretary of State respecting the increased fixed valuations for certain classes of goods adopted under the Calcutta tariff of April 1860, and to consider the feasibility of constructing a uniform table of tariff valuations for all India. Regarding the Calcutta tariff of April 1860, the committee concluded that the objections raised against it by interested parties in India and England were valid, that it was inequitable in principle, and that in respect to many of the chief articles of import it was excessive in its valuations. Having conceded this much, the committee went on to reject some of the charges levelled against the tariff by Lancashire interests and refuted with considerable technical detail statements made by the Manchester Chamber of Commerce and by the bleachers and dyers of Lancashire and Cheshire. The committee made three recommendations. First, it proposed that in order to avoid the inequalities in the incidence of the duties complained of both in India and England, valuations on grey cotton goods throughout India should be based on weight. This principle could not be applied to bleached, dyed, or fancy goods for which weight was not a test of value. The committee's second recommendation was that for these classes of goods duty should be assessed on their market price at the time of importation, rather than on a fixed tariff of valuations. The committee had also been asked to consider the feasibility of a uniform table of tariff valuations for all India, and its third recommendation was favourable to this idea. It submitted a proposed uniform table drawn up by Spooner in consultation with the mercantile community of Bombay.

Before submitting this report, the committee had held a meeting with representatives of most of the leading firms of Calcutta to sound their opinions, and had secured their unanimous approval of the proposed changes. Consequently the Government of India was able to accept the recommendations three days after receiving the committee's report.[39] Canning hastened to inform Wood, noting in particular the agreement of the merchants. He added that the grievances against the 10 per cent rate remained, but considered that this was not what the Manchester men had most pressed on Wood. On other points Canning hoped that the Secretary of State would be armed with a satisfactory answer to them. Canning also mentioned that according to Spooner the new cotton mills in Bombay were thriving and others were about to be set up. One Indian firm had even sent to America for a shipload of cotton to mix with Indian cotton. Spooner

[38]Report by the Customs Committee, dated 29 Oct. 1860, together with the revised Import Tariff of Valuations. Encl. in Government of India to Secretary of State, Letter no. 34 (Sep. Rev.), 2 Nov. 1860. Collections to Despatches (Sep. Rev.), V, no. 8.

[39]Government of India to Customs Committee, no. 2126, 1 Nov. 1860. Collections to Despatches (Sep. Rev.), V, no. 8.

thought the Indian mills were already equal to Manchester in all but the finer numbers of twist. Canning commented that if this were so, the duty on twist and yarn would have to be reduced for India's sake as well as for that of Manchester.[40] Wood was pleased with these developments. He agreed that Manchester had been most irked by the new tariff valuations of April 1860 rather than by the 10 per cent rate, while adding that more would be heard about the latter. He made it plain that he was prepared to accept a revenue tariff for India but not a tariff for protection: "You must remember that I never will acknowledge any claim to protection arising out of the existence of these high duties. If it suits Indian finances to abolish all import duties on yarn, or reduce them for revenue purposes, I shall not admit that the existence of mills at Bombay requires the maintenance of any duty."[41]

Manchester had won a victory on one of its two complaints: the system of tariff valuations. It was next to get its way over the rate of the import duty on yarns. Canning was prepared for a reduction of the duty, and Wood had suggested this to Laing before the latter left for India. He kept up the pressure after Laing's arrival in Calcutta. In February 1861 Wood had been visited by yet another deputation from Manchester, and although he exclaimed in exasperation that cotton manufacturers "talk more like fools than any set of men I have come across for a long time" he could not ignore them.[42] At the end of March he wrote to both Canning and Laing of the outcry that was going on in England over the cotton import duties, especially the 10 per cent on yarn. Those responsible for the outcry complained that the duty was ruining their export trade to India and for that very reason would cease to be a source of revenue. Wood said it would be "wise and politic ere long to reduce some of these indirect duties" and added that he doubted the need for the 10 per cent duty on yarn.[43] A month later he told Laing: "You can't keep the Import duties forever up at 10 per cent on all articles."[44] By then, however, Laing had decided to take the necessary action. On 27 April 1861, in presenting his budget to the Legislative Council he predicted a surplus for the year 1861–62 of £239,896 and announced a reduction in the import duty on yarn from 10 to 5 per cent.[45] In explanation Laing said that when the duty on yarn had been raised to 10 per cent in 1860 it was in the hope of securing an

[40]Canning to Wood, 2 Nov. 1860. Halifax Collection, I. O., Corresp., India.
[41]Wood to Canning, 7 Dec. 1860. Halifax Collection, I. O., Letter Books, V, p. 166–7.
[42]Ibid., 18 Feb. 1861, VI, p. 168.
[43]Wood to Canning, 26 Mar. 1861 (no. 1); Wood to Laing, 31 Mar. 1861 (no. 1). Halifax Collection, I. O., Letter Books, VII, p. 26 and p. 106.
[44]Ibid., 26 Apr. 1861 (no. 1), p. 194.
[45]India, *Legislative Council Proceedings,* vol. 7 (1861), p. 363. (In the two preceding years the deficits had amounted to £10,769,000 and £4,021,000 respectively. *Parl. Deb.,* 3rd ser., CLXVIII, col. 449.)

additional £67,000 in revenue. But the actual increase had been only half that amount. The duty on imported yarn ought not to be maintained at such a rate as to stimulate the growth of a protected interest. With impeccable free trade orthodoxy Laing declared:

> The principle of free trade is to impose taxes for purposes of Revenue only, and if yarn be a fit subject for taxation, there ought to be an excise on the native manufacture equal to the Customs duty on the imported article, unless the latter be so small in amount, that it would be palpably not worthwhile to establish a countervailing system of excise.[46]

Laing considered that with a rate of 5 per cent no excise was necessary, but that any higher rate would mean that untaxed native yarn was a protected article.

On the subject of the import duty on piece goods and other manufactures, Laing told the Legislative Council that he regretted he could not at once reduce the duties on these to 5 per cent; for such a reduction would mean a loss of £400,000 in revenue, which the Government could not afford under present circumstances. But he repeated that this was no reason why he could not at once deal with yarn, where the amount of revenue loss was small, the failure of the high duty evident, and the case urgent because mills were being constructed and machinery imported on the strength of the high duty. If Indian mills could compete with Manchester on equal terms, said Laing, then all well and good, but it would be unfair to induce the investment of capital in such mills on the strength of a protective duty which could only be maintained for a couple of years.[47] Wood was delighted with the reduction and told Laing that he was "charmed" by it.[48] Canning was less happy. He told the Secretary of State that the reduction of duty on yarns was "a bit of a flourish" and that he was not sure that his Government was justified in making it until a budget surplus had actually been achieved. "But I hope it may make a good impression at home. Laing wished to hold out something like a promise of reduction on piece goods, but I would not consent to that. There is a vast difference between £40,000 and £400,000."[49] Canning's caution was well founded, as Wood discovered when he examined the financial accounts of the Government of India. He then concluded that instead of a surplus as predicted by Laing, the Government of India would more likely face a deficit of £1 million. In announcing this in Parliament in July 1861 Wood nevertheless held out the hope that before long a reduction could be made in the duty on

---

[46]India, *Legislative Council Proceedings,* vol. 7 (1861), p. 351.
[47]Ibid., p. 352.
[48]Wood to Laing, 27 May 1861. Halifax Collection, I. O., Letter Books, VIII, p. 28.
[49]Canning to Wood, 4 May 1861. Halifax Collection, I. O., Corresp., India.

manufactured goods.[50] Laing, in fact, had already written to Wood asking his opinion on a proposed reduction in the duty on piece goods from 10 to 5 per cent. He believed that 10 per cent was too high and could not last, and said that a reduction would please all Lancashire if it could be done prudently.[51] But no further change could be made in the Indian tariff until the introduction of the next Indian budget in 1862. When that time approached, Lancashire prepared to exert renewed pressure.

In January 1862 the directors of the Manchester Chamber of Commerce again expressed their opinion that the duties on cotton yarns and fabrics imported into India were economically unsound. They said that such duties discouraged the export of raw cotton from India (an urgent problem due to the interruption of supplies from America, by then in the throes of civil war) and encouraged the development of a protective interest in India. The directors decided to send a deputation to Lord Elgin, who was about to leave England to succeed Canning as Governor-General, and present him with this opinion. They also resolved to make every effort to promote the early abolition of all duties on yarns and piece goods imported into India.[52] Soon after, Wood and Palmerston received a memorial from the cotton spinners, manufacturers, engineers, retail traders, operatives, and others of Over Darwen, a Lancashire manufacturing town the majority of whose population was dependent on the cotton trade.[53] Many memorials and petitions were received by the India Office from Lancashire in this period and this one provides a good example of the arguments used against the Indian cotton duties. The memorial stated that the duties were unsound in principle and opposed to the policy of free trade. They gave virtual protection to the manufacturers and spinners of India, who would become dependent on the tax-gatherer rather than upon their own exertions and the natural advantages they possessed. They directed capital into unnatural channels and increased the cost to the purchaser of Indian raw cotton. They inflicted great hardship on the many millions of poor Hindus whose clothing would be increased in price by more than 10 per cent since each trader would impose some extra fraction for interest and profit on the additional outlay required by the duties. Thus the poor Indian would be heavily mulcted on one of the only two necessities of his life. The memorial ended with a reference to the severe hardship caused by the cotton famine in Lancashire, and stated that if the Indian import duties were removed – in conjunction with other measures for the development of Indian

[50]*Parl. Deb.*, 3rd ser., CLXIV, col. 1513, 25 July 1861.

[51]Laing to Wood, 3 May 1861. Halifax Collection, I. O., Corresp., India.

[52]Manchester Chamber of Commerce to Lord Elgin, 15 Jan. 1862. Elgin Papers (India Office Library, MSS. Eur. F. 83). Miscellaneous Papers, no. 78 (1).

[53]The memorial was sent by Eccles Shorrock, J. P., to Secretary of State, 12 Feb. 1862. I. O., Rev. Dept., Home Corresp., Letters Rec., IV, no. 281.

resources – such a stimulus would be given to the export of Indian raw cotton to Britain that a crisis similar to the existing one would never occur again. A similar petition was drawn up at a public meeting of operatives held in the Spinners' Institute in Preston on 18 February 1862.[54] Deputations from Preston and other Lancashire towns then met in Fenton's Hotel, London, on 21 February. After their meeting, the joint deputation (which included the Mayor of Manchester) called upon Lord Palmerston, who was accompanied by Wood for the occasion.

Although Wood at first felt satisfied with his handling of the deputation, it soon became clear that he was wilting under the pressure being exerted on him. Wood told the deputation that the state of Indian finances required additional taxation, and that raising all the existing taxes, and imposing an income tax, as Wilson had done in 1860, was a fair method of raising revenue which nobody could complain about. He also said that he disliked high duties as much as the deputation did and that reduction would be made when the financial situation permitted it. Wood told Elgin with some satisfaction:

> They were overthrown as to the effect of the 10 per cent, when I showed them that they had exported as much in 1861 as in 1858, having, in the meantime, as they candidly admitted, sadly overstocked the market. All that they could say was, that they were sending out speculatively, as if they had not done so in former years, and to an excess in the last two years.[55]

But Wood's tone changed very quickly. A week later, on 3 March 1862, he wrote to Elgin expressing the wish that the duties on manufactured goods might be reduced to 5 per cent. There was, he said, a very strong feeling in the manufacturing districts about the matter. "They are suffering sensibly and although they talk absolute nonsense about it, and I don't

---

[54]Ibid., IV, no. 286.

[55]Wood to Elgin, 25 Feb. 1862. Halifax Collection, I. O., Letter Books, X, p. 44. In connection with Wood's statement about exports, a parliamentary return of all cotton exports to India for the period 1855–61 reveals the following salient figures:

Year	Piece Goods (Yd.)	Twist and Yarn (lb.)	Aggregate value of all manufactured cotton and yarn (£)
1858	791,647,041	36,782,583	11,358,656
1859	968,209,350	44,006,349	14,713,812
1860	825,076,246	30,723,214	12,425,736
1861	797,848,454	24,795,848	11,618,350

SOURCE: *Cotton: Return of the Cotton Goods exported to the British East Indies, and the Cotton imported therefrom, 1855 to 1861*, in *Parliamentary Papers*, LV (1862), No. 88, p. 627.

believe that the 10 per cent has had anything to do with the matter, it would be extremely popular to do it, and would soothe their feelings excited naturally enough by their sufferings."[56] Clearly, Wood was prepared to give in to Lancashire, even though he was convinced that the Indian import duties did not harm cotton exports from England. Wood thought that if exports were reduced the reason was that the Indian market had been immensely overstocked in 1859 and 1860.[57]

Wood had hardly written these words when he had to receive another deputation and memorial from the Manchester Chamber of Commerce. The memorial congratulated the Government for what it had done to expedite the supply of raw cotton from India, but complained of the "baneful effects" which had been produced by the increase in the duties levied on British yarns and manufactured goods imported into India. It asked for the immediate reduction and ultimate abolition of these duties.[58] Wood repeated that as soon as the state of Indian finances permitted, the duties would be reduced. He must have been glad to receive word not long after this meeting from Lord Elgin, who reported an anticipated balanced budget for the expiring financial year, 1861–62, and a predicted surplus for 1862–63 of upwards of £1 million. The question was how to employ that surplus. Elgin said there were three claims of an urgent kind: the first was the reduction of the import duty on cotton goods and other manufactures; the others were the abolition of the 2 per cent income tax imposed by Wilson in 1860, and improvement of education and public works. As far as the import duties were concerned, Elgin believed that British manufacturers exaggerated the effect which these duties had in stimulating the sale of native goods and checking the demand for imports. Moreover, there was a good deal of jealousy in India of financial proposals which were allegedly advocated in a purely English interest. Nevertheless, Elgin thought there were weighty reasons in favour of reducing the duties as soon as possible to the old rate of 5 per cent. He considered there was no doubt that the existing duties did have some protective effect, and believed that even if this were not quite so obvious, the discontent and ill will which the duties occasioned in England were evils of no small magnitude which it was very desirable to abate. Therefore those who wished the Indian import duties lowered had a strong claim to be heard if the Government had a surplus.[59]

[56]Wood to Elgin, 3 Mar. 1862. Halifax Collection, I. O., Letter Books, X, p. 44.

[57]Ibid., 12 Mar. 1862, pp. 86–88. Wood was correct in this assumption. See Eugene A. Brady, "A Reconsideration of the Lancashire 'Cotton Famine'," *Agricultural History*, XXXVII (1963), pp. 156–62.

[58]*Proceedings of the Manchester Chamber of Commerce*, 13 Mar. 1862.

[59]Elgin to Wood, 9 Apr. 1862. Elgin Papers, Letters from the Governor-General to the Secretary of State, I, pp. 42–47.

In fact, the decision had already been made to lower the duties and this was announced in the Legislative Council on 16 April 1862, when Laing presented his budget for 1862–63. He said that he anticipated a surplus of £1,428,683 for the year, or £900,000 after extra allocations for education and public works. He explained how the Government proposed to deal with this surplus. The increased duty on piece goods and yarns produced less than £500,000; at the rate of importation for the previous nine months, the difference between a 10 per cent and a 5 per cent duty was not quite £450,000 a year. Therefore it was time to remit the extra duty imposed to meet an emergency. Laing admitted that proposals had been made, notably by J. P. Grant, now the Lieutenant-Governor of Bengal, that the higher duty should be retained as part of the regular financial system. The Government of India did not accept this for two reasons. The first was related to Britain's imperial interests. Laing said that the duty applied almost exclusively to British manufactures. "Now, as long as England and India remain parts of our great Empire, it is impossible to apply precisely the same rules as if they were separate and independent countries."[60] Laing noted that England had completely given up all pretensions to exact a tribute from India and all claim on a monopoly of the Indian market, and that "speculative reasoners" had even argued that Great Britain would be better off without its empire. He said that this was an opinion which no practical statesman would for a moment entertain, and affirmed that the extension of commerce was the most direct and palpable advantage derived by England from the possession of India. A heavy Indian import duty on British goods was therefore nearly equivalent to a transit duty between different parts of the same empire. Laing underlined his argument as follows:

> To those who argue this point on abstract grounds, and overlook the practical considerations arising from our actual position with regard to England, I would simply put two questions. – Do you believe that if Ireland found it was more convenient to tax Manchester goods than to levy a Poor Rate, she would be allowed to do so? – Or do you believe that if it were found that 25 per cent would give India a better revenue than 10 per cent, we could raise the Duty to that amount with the slightest chance of retaining it?[61]

There could have been no clearer statement of free trade attitudes to empire than that.

The second argument was related to the principles of free trade. Assuming that clothing was a proper subject for taxation, asked Laing, on

[60]India, *Legislative Council Proceedings,* new series, vol. I (1862), p. 66.
[61]Loc. cit.

what principle could a duty be imposed on imported clothing when none was levied on home-produced clothing? "It is the old question of the Corn Laws over again." Free trade meant that taxes should be levied for revenue purposes only, and every customs duty on an imported article should be balanced by an excise duty on a similar home-produced article unless the import duty was so moderate it did not seriously impede trade. Laing said the Government could not dispense with customs duties on imports generally, and there was no reasonable objection to the old rate of 5 per cent on manufactured goods. But an import duty of 10 per cent required a countervailing excise duty, and the Government did not think this desirable because it did not wish to discourage manufactures in India. It also wanted to avoid bestowing on India the fatal boon of protection. Laing concluded that the extra duty of 5 per cent on imported cotton goods did in the long run raise prices to the consumer by an equivalent amount, and that its reduction would probably stimulate trade. For these reasons the Government intended to reduce the import duties on piece goods and yarns immediately to the old rates of 5 and $3\frac{1}{2}$ per cent respectively.

The fact that similar reductions were not made in the duties on other imports is a good indication that the lowering of the cotton duties was really attributable to pressure from Lancashire, and was carried out in the interests of the Lancashire cotton industry. As Laing frankly admitted: "The same arguments for reduction as in the case of Piece Goods, do not apply to other articles of the Tariff which are not extensively produced in India as well as imported."[62]

In India the decrease in the cotton duties did not pass without protest. Elgin told Wood that the general and popular feeling in the local press was that the reduction was simply a boon to Manchester manufacturers, and that the interests of India were being sacrificed to those of a class in England.[63] This, of course, was perfectly true. Laing knew that Manchester would say that the entire 10 per cent should have been repealed, but he considered that if corn could pay one shilling a quarter in England, cotton might pay 5 per cent in India.[64] In England, Wood was naturally pleased at the reduction, although he already anticipated further demands from Lancashire. He warned Laing early in May 1862 that there was "a little cloud on the horizon that we may be pressed to put an excise duty on cotton goods made in India equivalent to the customs duties on English

[62]India, *Legislative Council Proceedings*, n.s., I (1862), pp. 67–68. The reductions became law as Act XI of 1862.

[63]Elgin to Wood, 9 Apr. 1862. Elgin Papers, Letters from the Governor-General to the Secretary of State, I, pp. 62–63. The agents of many British manufacturing houses immediately petitioned to have the reductions postponed so that they could sell off the stocks of cotton goods they had on hand.

[64]Laing to Wood, 18 Apr. 1862. Halifax Collection, I. O., Corresp., India.

goods."[65] He feared the development of a protective spirit in India in view of a petition from Bombay merchants for the continuance of the 10 per cent duties, and said he would not tolerate this. Nor would he surrender any duty needed for revenue purposes simply because it might, to a small extent, be protective.[66]

Wood made this point because of his continuing concern over the state of Indian finances. In June he sent a despatch to the Government of India rebuking it for serious errors in the financial estimates for 1862–63. Making allowances for these errors, the Secretary of State estimated a deficit of £284,086 for the year, instead of Laing's predicted surplus of nearly one and a half million. He therefore directed reductions in expenditures, particularly for education and public works, but expressed full approval of the reduction in the cotton duties.[67] Wood had every reason to stress the latter point. Within a fortnight of sending this despatch, he told Elgin that he was overdone with deputations from Lancashire asking for abolition of the duties on piece goods. Their reason was distress in the manufacturing districts. He had told the deputations that they had nothing to expect beyond the reduction to 5 per cent.[68] Privately, Wood thought that although there was undoubted distress in Lancashire, it caused little real concern among the masters; for they had stocked the Indian market to excess and, in many cases, stood to lose more by working their mills than by stopping production.[69]

But by the beginning of 1863 the position had changed. In England, conditions in the cotton textile industry improved and distress in Lancashire diminished. In India, the demand for raw cotton for export had led to a sharp rise in the price of cotton goods. In January 1863 Laing's successor as Finance Member, Sir Charles Trevelyan, stated that in consequence of this price rise the 5 per cent duty on grey goods (the largest item of cotton imports) had become a practical 3 per cent in terms of the tariff valuation fixed in November 1860.[70] Trevelyan had the power to restore the tariff price to its proper relation to the market price but he decided not to use it.[71] He wanted instead to reduce the general rate of import duties from 10 per cent to the level of 5 per cent enjoyed by cotton piece goods. He was concerned by what he called "the great embarrassment

---

[65]Wood to Laing, 10 May 1862. Halifax Collection, I. O., Letter Books, X, p. 234.
[66]Ibid., 19 May 1862, p. 240.
[67]Secretary of State to Government of India, Despatch no. 83 (Financial), 9 June 1862. Eventually it turned out that there was a surplus of £1,827,000 for 1862–63. *Parl. Deb.*, 3rd ser., CLXXVI, col. 1809, 21 July 1864.
[68]Wood to Elgin, 18 June 1862. Halifax Collection, I. O., Letter Books, X, p. 308.
[69]Wood to Sir William Denison (Governor of Madras), 10 July 1862. Halifax Collection, I. O., Letter Books XI, p. 16.
[70]Trevelyan to Wood, 21 Jan. 1863. Halifax Collection, I. O., Corresp., India.
[71]Ibid., 27 Jan. 1863.

of India's trade" – the excess of exports over imports, which had grown worse because of the urgent demand for Indian raw cotton. In his view it would be to England's advantage to substitute goods for bullion in her trading relations with India.[72] Throughout 1863 the price of cotton goods rose still higher, creating a further imbalance between the tariff price and the market price in terms of the 1860 valuations. Accordingly, in April 1864 Trevelyan at last raised the tariff valuations on cotton goods, while at the same time reducing the general rate of import duties from 10 to 7½ per cent.[73]

Trevelyan's action led to an outcry from Lancashire. The Manchester Chamber of Commerce at once sent a memorial to the India Office requesting the total abolition of the cotton duties and claiming that the revised valuations announced by Trevelyan represented a substantial increase in the amount of duty levied on imported cotton goods. It also complained that this represented additional protection for Indian cotton mills.[74] For the moment the India Office was able to deflect Lancashire's attack by reminding its representatives that cotton piece goods and yarns enjoyed an advantage over all other imported goods by being admitted at lower rates.[75] Lancashire then tried a new approach, emphasizing the wider problems of Anglo-Indian trade relations and setting its special pleas within this context. It took up Trevelyan's arguments about the great disproportion between India's exports and imports. India's trade was "hampered and harassed" by the difficulty of obtaining specie to pay for the difference, the Manchester Chamber of Commerce argued, and the shipment of bullion to India raised discount rates to the detriment of the general trade of the country. The only remedy was to remove all impediments to the expansion of India's import trade, particularly the cotton duties.[76] To press the point home, the chamber sent a deputation to see Trevelyan's successor as Finance Member, W. N. Massey, prior to his departure for India early in 1865. They emphasized to him the "impolicy and injustice" of import duties on cotton goods.[77]

All this pressure began to have some effect on the Secretary of State. When Trevelyan returned home after his resignation from the Governor-

---

[72]Trevelyan to Elgin, 11 Apr. 1863. Elgin Papers, Letters from Members of Council, p. 427.

[73]India, *Legislative Council Proceedings*, n.s., III (1864), p. 148.

[74]India, *Legislative Council Proceedings*, n.s., III (1864), pp. 13–48. Trevelyan balanced this increase in the tariff valuations on cotton goods by reducing the general import duty from 10 to 7½ per cent. This was still higher than the import duties on piece goods and yarns.

[75]Assistant Under-Secretary of State to Manchester Chamber of Commerce, 21 July 1864. I. O., Rev. Dept., Home Corresp., Letters Sent, II, no. 270.

[76]Manchester Chamber of Commerce to Secretary of State, 1 Sept. 1864. I. O., Rev. Dept., Home Corresp., Letters Rec., VI, no. 541.

[77]*Proceedings of the Manchester Chamber of Commerce*, 22 Feb. 1865.

General's Council, Wood asked him to draw up a memorandum on the question of competition between cotton goods manufactured in Lancashire and in India.[78] Trevelyan considered that the balance of advantages lay with Lancashire – cheap capital, machinery, fuel, and skilled superintendence; the Indian manufacturer had the sole advantage of cheap raw material, but it was of inferior quality. He thought that the Indian mill industry was in competition with the Indian handloom weaver rather than with Lancashire. This was an additional reason for not imposing an excise duty on cotton goods produced in India, because such a tax, unless it were imposed on the weavers as well as the mill-owners, would give them an advantage which would prolong their existence as a class. Trevelyan, however, looked forward to their disappearance, a development which he thought would benefit both England and India. India would benefit because competition from machine-made goods would force the weavers to give up their craft and turn to agriculture; agricultural output would then rise because of the increased supply of labour. England would benefit because makers of cloth would be converted into consumers of Lancashire goods.[79] Trevelyan also recommended that, before making up his mind on the cotton duties, Wood should wait and see the results of the fresh stimulus which had been given to English industry by the termination of the war in America.

Trevelyan's arguments seemed to be borne out by the rise in British cotton exports from 1864 (see Table 2.2). The trend was upwards, with exports to India holding up well in relation to total exports.[80] Wood therefore saw no reason to give way to pressure from Lancashire for the abolition of the cotton duties, and no further changes in the duties were made during the remainder of his tenure.

Wood's unexpected resignation as Secretary of State for India in February 1866 encouraged the cotton manufacturers to return to the attack. At the end of March the Manchester Chamber of Commerce sent a deputation to argue Lancashire's case with Wood's successor, Earl de Grey. The deputation contended that the Indian import duties gave protection to the Indian mill industry, and elaborate figures were produced to prove India's "unfair" advantage over Lancashire in manufacturing yarn and cloth.[81] De Grey repeated the customary arguments about India's financial condition which made it difficult for the Government to surrender

---

[78]The memorandum is enclosed in Trevelyan to Wood, 21 June 1865. I. O., Corresp., India.

[79]India, *Legislative Council Proceedings*, n.s., II (1863), p. 79.

[80]The unusually high value of British cotton exports to India in 1859 was the result of an attempt by British exporters to flood the Indian market that year. See Eugene A. Brady, "A Reconsideration of the Lancashire 'Cotton Famine'." *Agricultural History*, XXXVII (1963), pp. 158–60.

[81]*Proceedings of the Manchester Chamber of Commerce*, 4 Apr. 1866.

Table 2.2

Exports of Yarn and Piece Goods from Great Britain, 1858–72

Year	Total Exports (£ millions)	Exports to India (£ millions)	Exports to India as per cent of total exports
1858	43.0	11.4	26.5
1859	48.1	14.7	30.6
1860	52.0	12.4	23.8
1861	46.8	11.6	24.8
1862	36.8	10.2	27.7
1863	47.6	9.6	20.2
1864	54.8	11.9	21.7
1865	57.2	13.2	23.1
1866	74.6	13.8	18.5
1867	70.8	15.7	22.2
1868	67.7	17.7	26.1
1869	67.9	18.9	27.8
1870	66.4	16.3	24.6
1871	73.4	19.0	25.9
1872	80.2	17.5	21.9

SOURCES: *Statistical Abstract for the United Kingdom in Each of the Last Fifteen Years from 1858 to 1872*, in *Parliamentary Papers*, LXIX (1873), C. 833, Table 25; *Return of All Cotton Exports to India for the Period 1855–1861*, ibid., LV (1862), No. 88; *Statistical Abstract of British India, 1862–71*, ibid., LXIII (1872), C. 587, Table 18; *Statistical Abstract of British India, 1863–72*, ibid., LXIX (1873), C. 870, Table 19.

sources of revenue. The fact was that, as will be shown later, while Lancashire was asking the Government to give up the cotton duties, it was also demanding expenditure on railways, roads, canals, and irrigation projects designed to open up India to British exports and develop her as a source of raw materials. This drew an exasperated comment from the Governor-General, Sir John Lawrence:

> Everyone calls for more and more expenditure, while none are for more taxation, and many desire a reduction of these burthens. In the conflict of views and interests it is not easy to decide what course we should pursue. I see that the Manchester men press for a reduction or rather for the abolition of the import duties on cotton goods which they estimate at £600,000 per annum. Assuredly we are not in a position to do this. Indeed our customs for all India, some $2\frac{1}{2}$ millions per annum, are by no means what such a country should yield.[82]

But if the Government of India, supported by the Secretary of State, was not prepared to abolish the cotton duties, it was ready to make concessions to Lancashire in the form of lower tariff valuations on imported

[82]Sir John Lawrence to Earl de Grey, 5 March 1866. John Lawrence Collection (India Office Library, MSS. Eur. F. 90), Letters to the Secretary of State, VIII, no. 12.

cotton goods. In March 1866 it set up a committee to revise the valuations, and reductions were made in 1867 and again in 1869. This was done in response to complaints from Lancashire that the fall in cotton prices following the termination of the American Civil War had raised the incidence of the duty. For a time these concessions muted the opposition to the cotton duties, but when trade conditions took a downward turn in 1874 the Lancashire manufacturers returned to the attack. They charged that the retention of the 5 per cent duty on imported cotton goods represented a protective advantage for the growing Indian mill industry and they were determined to have it abolished.

On 31 January 1874 the Manchester Chamber of Commerce sent a memorial to the India Office complaining that Indian manufacturers proposed to import long-stapled cotton from America or Egypt, on which there was no duty, in order to manufacture the finer qualities of cloth in competition with Lancashire goods, on which there was an import duty of 5 per cent. In fairness to the English manufacturer and in the interests of the Indian consumer the cotton duties should be abolished, they argued. Lord Salisbury, the Secretary of State in the new Conservative government which had just come to power, agreed with these arguments and informed the Government of India that it should remove the duties whenever the state of Indian finances allowed.[83] In November 1874, a committee was set up in India to look into the tariff question. It rejected. Manchester's demand for the abolition of the cotton duties on the ground that Indian mills manufactured coarse cloth only. India possessed certain natural capabilities for producing low quality goods which would probably secure for her the trade in such goods, even if the duty were removed. Lancashire, on the other hand, exported only fine quality goods to India, where they met practically no competition. It was therefore unreasonable to demand the abolition of the import duty on such goods, especially when the loss to the Indian revenues was taken into account.[84]

The Government of India accepted these conclusions and in the Tariff Bill which it introduced into the Legislative Council on 5 August 1875 it reduced the import duties on a number of articles other than cotton goods and imposed a duty of 5 per cent on raw cotton.[85] Salisbury was annoyed at what he considered the unilateral action of the Government of India, taken without consulting him, and he warned that he might have to disallow the new measure. He admitted that Lancashire's fears of the

[83]Memorial of the Manchester Chamber of Commerce, encl. in Secretary of State to Government of India, Despatch no. 2 (Sep. Rev.), 26 March 1874.

[84]Report of the Tariff Committee, 27 Feb. 1875, encl. in Government of India to Secretary of State, Letter no. 15 (Sep. Rev.), 16 Aug. 1875.

[85]India, *Legislative Council Proceedings*, n.s., XIV (1875), pp. 173 ff. The bill was passed as Act XVI of 1875 on the same day.

protective effect of the 5 per cent duty on piece goods and yarn were exaggerated but there were political objections to it which could not be ignored. He therefore urged the Viceroy, Lord Northbrook to remove the cotton duties as soon as the state of India's finances permitted.[86] But this despatch reached India after the new tariff legislation had been enacted. The Home and Indian governments were clearly on a collision course; in order to head off a clash, Salisbury sent the Permanent Under-Secretary of State for India, Sir Louis Mallet, to discuss the matter personally with the Viceroy.

Before Mallet ever reached India, Salisbury had disallowed those portions of the Tariff Act which applied to the import duties. His reasons were twofold. First, the retention of the duty on cotton imports was inconsistent with the British policy of free trade, which the British government could not set aside without special cause in any part of the empire under its direct control. The second reason was purely political: if abolition of the duties were long postponed, the issue would become a subject of controversy between interests far more powerful and embittered than those currently disputing it.[87] Therefore, he concluded, the Government of India must enact immediately legislation to amend its Tariff Act.

The Government of India did not give way without a fight. Northbrook pointed out that in 1874–75 the revenue raised by the cotton duties had produced £882,712. The loss of this revenue could be made good only by additional taxation. Northbrook clearly stated that it was the Government of India's "duty to consider the subject with regard to the interests of India; we do not consider that the removal of the import duty upon cotton manufactures is consistent with these interests. . . ."[88] Northbrook followed up with a Minute signed by all the members of his Council. In it they vigorously protested against Salisbury's argument that they should give way to the pressure of the Lancashire cotton interests lest these interests should make some greater demand in the future. They asserted the contrary view in strong language, echoing the views expressed by J. P. Grant nearly twenty years earlier:

> We think it our duty to submit our earnest protest against the principle that the taxation of India is to be regulated under pressure from powerful classes in England, whose private interest may not be the interest of India, and with regard to the principle established in England and for England, and without ascertaining by communication with the responsible Government in India the policy or financial bearing of the measure or the views and sentiments of our Indian subjects.[89]

[86]Secretary of State to Government of India, Despatch no. 6 (Sep. Rev.), 15 July 1875.
[87]Secretary of State to Government of India, Despatch no. 51 (Legislative), 11 Nov. 1875.
[88]Government of India to Secretary of State, Letter no. 3 (Sep. Rev.), 25 Feb. 1876.
[89]Government of India to Secretary of State, Letter no. 19 (Public), 31 March 1876.

Shortly afterwards, however, Northbrook resigned for personal reasons.[90] His successor, Lord Lytton, was quite amenable to instructions from London to abolish the duties as soon as possible.[91] But Lytton found that this was more difficult than he had thought. The Afghan question, an exchange crisis caused by the fall in the value of silver, and famine caused by the failure of the monsoon made it impossible for the Government of India to give up the revenue derived from the cotton duties. The question was therefore held over until 1877 when the issue was raised in the House of Commons. On 10 July, two Manchester members of Parliament, H. Birley (a Conservative) and Jacob Bright (a Liberal) brought in a motion calling for outright repeal of the cotton duties, which they said were protective and contrary to sound commercial policy.[92] Bright brought out clearly Lancashire's principal objections to the cotton duties. He pointed out that in 1871 there were only 11 factories in Bombay presidency and in 1875 there were 41. Moreover, they were beginning to expand their production from coarse to fine fabrics. Yet India was able to import machinery free of duty and such imports had risen in value from £300,000 in 1870 to £1,500,000 in 1875. Bright asked what India's value to Great Britain was and his answer was a restatement of the "free trade" attitude to empire: the glory of its possession, the occasion it gave to civilize "inferior" peoples, the employment it gave to those in the civil and military services, and the "belief that our trade with India was more secure than it could be if India were in other hands. This last consideration had great weight with practical minds."[93] The parliamentary Under-Secretary of State for India, Lord George Hamilton, added an amendment "so soon as the finances of India will permit" and thus amended the motion passed without a division. In view of the poor shape of India's finances, even Salisbury agreed that this was not the moment to reduce the tariffs.[94]

However, concessions were made to Lancashire early in 1878, when coarse goods were exempted from duty. Lancashire was not appeased by this gesture and continued to press for total repeal. With a general election in the offing, Conservative party politicians feared a loss of up to 14 seats in Lancashire unless the cotton interests were convinced that the duties would be at least progressively reduced.[95] Cranbrook knew that the

[90]He did not resign because of conflict with Salisbury over the cotton duties. See Dalit Gujral, "Sir Louis Mallet's Mission to Lord Northbrook on the Question of the Cotton Duties," *Journal of Indian History*, XXXIX (1961), pp. 485–87.

[91]Secretary of State to Government of India, Despatch no. 9 (Sep. Rev.), 31 May 1876.

[92]*Parl. Deb.*, 3rd ser., CCXXXV, col. 1085, 10 July 1877.

[93]Ibid., col. 1093.

[94]Salisbury to Lytton, 19 Oct. 1877. Lytton Papers (India Office Library, MSS. Eur. E. 218), vol. 516/2, fol. 42.

[95]Cranbrook to Lytton, 4 Feb., 15 Feb., and 3 Mar. 1897. Lytton Papers, 516/4, fols. 39–40, 51–56, 85–90. Cranbrook succeeded Salisbury as Secretary of State for India on 2 Apr. 1878.

general trade depression caused by the depreciation of silver – not the cotton duties – was the main factor affecting British cotton exports to India. But the political necessity of appeasing a powerful pressure-group was paramount. In March 1879, despite strong opposition from his Council, Lytton sanctioned a further reduction of import duties on cotton manufactures, although he was not able to achieve total repeal. But this was not long delayed; for in 1882 the Government of India abolished all general import duties.

In public, the justification for repeal of the duties was the theory of free trade. The Finance Member, Evelyn Baring, explained to the Legislative Council that India, as a result of her connection with England, had a right to benefit from English experience and English economic history, which showed the benefits of a free trade policy. Baring further argued that the abolition of the duties would meet the contention of Sir Charles Trevelyan in 1864 "that the great embarrassment of the trade of India has always been the want of imports to meet the vast quantity of exportable produce which the country is capable of sending forth."[96] Finally, Baring claimed that removal of restrictions on trade would stimulate railway construction. Privately, however, both Baring and the Viceroy, Lord Ripon, agreed that it was political pressure rather than fiscal arguments which had led to general repeal of the duties, and that India had been sacrificed on the altar of Manchester.[97]

So ended a quarter-century of conflict between Lancashire and India over the cotton duties.[98] The Government of India had imposed them because of financial necessity and had argued for their retention on the same ground. Lancashire opposed them for two main reasons. One was that the duties, particularly those on yarn, would give an advantage to the Indian handloom industry. Competition from the handloom industry would reduce the market for Lancashire's products, and it would also hinder the development of agriculture by retaining labour in the industrial sector which could more usefully be employed in growing cotton for export to Lancashire. The other reason was that the duty on imported cloth gave protection to the developing Indian cotton industry. At first, Lancashire

[96]India, *Legislative Council Proceedings*, n.s., XXI (1882), p. 228. See also p. 28, *n.* 72.

[97]Amales Tripathi, "Manchester, India Office and the Tariff Controversy, 1858–1882," Indian Historica Records Commission, *Proceedings*, XXXVI, pt. 2 (1961), p. 19.

[98]This was not the end of the story. In 1894 the Government of India, again under financial strain, reimposed the import duties but at first exempted cotton goods. When the duties were extended to cotton goods, pressure from Lancashire first caused a countervailing excise duty to be levied on Indian-produced goods and then abolition of the duty on yarn and reduction of the duty on piece goods to $3\frac{1}{2}$ per cent, although the general rate remained at 5 per cent. See Peter Harnetty, "The Indian Cotton Duties Controversy, 1894–1896," *English Historical Review*, LXXVII (1962), pp. 684–702. Not until after the reforms of 1919 did India gain a measure of tariff autonomy.

was appeased by reduction of the duties and adjustments in the system of tariff valuations. But the rapid development of Indian cotton mills in the 1870s, combined with a trade slump at home, caused Lancashire to press for total repeal of the duties, an object which they secured by 1882.

Lancashire's arguments against the import duties were frequently dressed up in the theoretical ideology of free trade but the underlying reason was that stated by Laing in the Legislative Council on 16 April 1862. The advantage to Britain of her control of India was the opportunity it gave to extend British trade with her dependency. This included the power to manipulate the tariff in the interests of British industry. In other words, Laing was expressing the mercantilist view that dependencies exist for the benefit of the metropolitan state. The burden of Lancashire's complaint in the mid-nineteenth century was that the Indian import duties meant that India was not completely fulfilling that role. It followed that the duties must be repealed.

3

THE COTTON SUPPLY QUESTION

"I DO BELIEVE," said John Bright in the House of Commons on 6 May 1847, "that what potatoes are to Ireland, cotton is to Lancashire." He was repeating a warning which had been made as early as 1828 by a Liverpool correspondent of the Board of Trade who had cautioned the cotton industry about the dangers of its excessive dependence on the United States for the supply of its raw material.[1] Bright's statement was prompted by the "cotton famine" of 1846 which brought home to the cotton industry the desirability of securing an alternative source of supply. This would not only insure the industry against future interruptions in the supply of its raw material but would also lower cotton prices by breaking the monopoly enjoyed by American producers. India was seen as the best alternative and Bright secured the appointment of a parliamentary committee in 1848 to find out why the East India Company had failed to make India into a major exporter of cotton.

This was the opening round in a campaign, extending over the next quarter of a century, to secure government action to improve the Indian cotton supply picture. The chief source of Lancashire pressure for such action was the Manchester Chamber of Commerce, reinforced in 1857 by

[1]W. O. Henderson, *The Lancashire Cotton Famine* (Manchester: Manchester University Press, 1934), p. 35.

the Cotton Supply Association.[2] After the failure of Bright's parliamentary committee to secure any positive results, the Chamber of Commerce held a special meeting early in 1850 to consider the question. Its president, Thomas Bazley, M.P., referred to the fact that the United States, which supplied more than 90 per cent of Lancashire's raw cotton, had recently raised its tariffs to the disadvantage of British manufacturers. Bazley struck two themes which were to form a persistent element in Lancashire's attitude to the cotton supply problem in the mid-nineteenth century. One was that the object should be to diversify sources of supply, not to check the quantity of cotton coming from America. In other words, India would be a back-up source, the existence of which would hold American cotton prices down and protect Lancashire against a failure of the American supply. The other was the complaint that the Government of India was indifferent to both British and Indian interests in ignoring the possibilities of increasing the output of cotton by encouraging its cultivation in India.[3] Thus, although normally adhering to the principles of *laissez-faire*, Lancashire was willing to set aside these principles in order to promote India's development as an agricultural economy, with which its own prosperity was closely connected.

Lancashire's attitude was expressed in a petition which the Manchester Chamber of Commerce subsequently sent to the Prime Minister. It deplored Great Britain's dependence on a single source of raw cotton, condemned the East India Company's failure to secure any increase in the production of cotton in India, called for a searching inquiry into the causes of this failure, and demanded the despatch of a commission of inquiry to India. The demand for a commission of inquiry was repeated in the House of Commons in a motion presented by John Bright on 18 June 1850. When Bright's motion was defeated, the Manchester Chamber of Commerce appointed its own representative, the barrister Alexander Mackay, to go to India in 1851 to inquire into the obstacles preventing the increase of cotton production in India and the failure of efforts to improve the quality of Indian cotton. Mackay spent a year in India touring the chief cotton districts. His findings, published posthumously, were highly critical of the East India Company.[4] In the field of material progress, Mackay claimed that India was still as backward as when Alexander the Great crossed the Indus.

[2]For the relationship between the Manchester Chamber of Commerce and the Cotton Supply Association, founded in Manchester in 1857 to encourage the growth of cotton wherever possible, see Arthur W. Silver, *Manchester Men and Indian Cotton, 1847–1872* (Manchester: Manchester University Press, 1966), pp. 100–01.

[3]*Proceedings of the Manchester Chamber of Commerce* (Manchester Central Reference Library), vol. 5 (1849–58), 17 Jan. 1850.

[4]Alexander Mackay, *Western India* (London: N. Cooke, 1853).

When Mackay's criticisms appeared, the renewal of the East India Company's charter was due for debate in Parliament. The President of the Board of Control, Sir Charles Wood, defended the Company's record but privately he thought the Lancashire interests were right in their desire to diversify their sources of cotton supply and he agreed with them that India was the obvious alternative to America.[5] The Company's charter was renewed over the strenuous opposition of a group of Lancashire members of Parliament, led by John Bright, who represented Manchester, and organized as the Indian Reform Society.[6] Thereafter, the Manchester Chamber of Commerce kept up its pressure for increased government activity to develop India as a source of cotton. It made its views known to the Governor-General designate, Lord Canning, before he left for India late in 1855.[7] Then in 1857 it petitioned the House of Commons, pointing out the dangers of Great Britain's dependence on the United States for supplies of raw cotton.[8] An inconclusive debate on the subject of the growth of cotton in India was held in Parliament on 23 June 1857 but, soon after, the news of the Indian Rebellion diverted attention to political issues.

For the next two and one-half years, the Manchester Chamber of Commerce and the Cotton Supply Association kept up constant pressure on the government for measures to turn India into a major supplier of the raw material. The approach of civil war in America lent new urgency to Lancashire's interest in Indian cotton. Delegates to the annual general meeting of the Manchester Chamber of Commerce on 21 January 1861 again expressed fears for the continued supply of cotton, 80 per cent of which still came from the United States, and they decided to call a conference of deputations from various Chambers of Commerce, Members of Parliament, and other persons interested in the trade of India, to consider the matter. This conference met in Manchester on 31 January and passed a number of resolutions drafted the previous day by the directors of the local Chamber of Commerce.[9] They expressed great uneasiness about the financial position of India, especially the high level of military expenditure there, but at the same time they suggested that a loan should be raised for the resumption and completion of public works suspended in the previous November. They also urged a reduction of import duties, and called for

[5]Wood to Dalhousie, 24 Mar. and 8 Apr. 1853. Halifax Collection, India Board, Letter Books, III, pp. 44 and 52.

[6]R. J. Moore, *Sir Charles Wood's Indian Policy, 1853–66* (Manchester: Manchester University Press, 1966), pp. 125–28.

[7]Bazley to Canning, 17 Nov. 1855, enclosing an address from the directors of the Manchester Chamber of Commerce. Canning Papers, 114 (Papers on Miscellaneous Subjects), no. 978.

[8]*Proceedings of the Manchester Chamber of Commerce*, 22 June 1857.

[9]*Proceedings of the Manchester Chamber of Commerce*, vol. 6 (1858–67), 30 Jan. 1861.

reform of the Indian contract law and the system of land tenure.[10] The Conference then adjourned to London, where it continued its discussions immediately after the opening of the parliamentary session. A memorial based on the resolutions passed in Manchester was presented to the Secretary of State for India, Sir Charles Wood, on 21 February and to the Prime Minister, Lord Palmerston, on the following day. During an interview with the Secretary of State, the president of the Manchester Chamber of Commerce emphasized the danger that Lancashire's supply of cotton might be cut off because of events in America. India alone could make up the deficiency, but lack of roads and efficient means of transport largely prevented her cotton from reaching the ports. The only remedy was to hasten railway construction, which could not be carried out by private enterprise. Government, he argued, "as the owner of the soil of India," should carry out works of improvement and should raise a loan of from £30 to £40 million for the purpose. Such a proposal was quite unacceptable to Sir Charles Wood, who was greatly concerned at this time over India's financial difficulties in the wake of the Mutiny. Moreover, he had just borrowed £3 million for further railway construction, an example of government investment in India's economic development which apparently astonished the deputation he had received.[11] Further borrowing was impossible while India was, in Wood's opinion, "drifting to bankruptcy."[12]

Government response to Lancashire's demand for action was not, however, entirely negative. On 28 February 1861 the Government of India published a Resolution announcing the policy it was prepared to follow in order to encourage cotton cultivation in India.[13] Two principles were laid down. First, the Government would not sanction any measure which placed it in the position of the private capitalist, cultivator, or speculator, or which in any way interfered with private enterprise. Therefore, all schemes to stimulate cotton cultivation by direct government action, such as establishing model farms or experimental cultivation conducted by officials, were out of the question. Second, any proposal must stimulate cotton production and export during the *next* season (1861–62). This excluded such long-term improvements as railway and canal construction.

Subject to these limitations, the Government suggested a number of ways in which official action could indirectly stimulate increased production

10Proceedings of the Manchester Chamber of Commerce, 30 Jan. 1861.
11Wood to Canning, 26 Feb. 1861, Halifax Collection, India Office, Letter Books, VI, p. 182.
12The phrase was used in Wood to Canning, 4 Mar. 1861. Halifax Collection, I. O., Letter Books, VI, p. 232.
13Resolution of the Governor-General in Council in the Home Dept., 28 Feb. 1861. Supplement to the *Calcutta Gazette*, LXXI, no. 14, 2 Mar. 1861.

of cotton and improve the means of getting it to port. An immediate increase in production would depend on the rapidity with which information regarding demand and prices in England could be communicated to Indian producers, and on the removal of impediments to rapid communication between the growers and purchasers of cotton in the districts and the merchants at the ports who exported it.[14] The Government therefore proposed that agents of the mercantile communities in the major ports should visit the interior and do their best to eliminate native middlemen, and it offered special facilities to aid their banking arrangements in those parts of the country where there were no banks. The Government thought it could best aid the merchants by improving the means of bringing cotton to port and it asked the local governments to take immediate steps to have the lines of traffic between the cotton-producing districts and the ports of shipment examined and reported on. It offered special grants for simple works, particularly the improvement of country cart and bullock tracks, and suggested that government officers employed on such works should be accompanied by a member of the commercial community whose expenses would be paid from public funds.

This limited view of the role government should play in encouraging cotton cultivation received full support from the Secretary of State, although he termed "objectionable" the Government of India's proposal to defray out of the public revenue the travelling or other expenses of persons deputed by commercial communities, and said that this ought not to be repeated.[15] At the same time, Wood was anxious to convince Lancashire that the Government really wished to encourage cotton cultivation in India. He therefore asked Sir George Clerk, the Governor of Bombay, to try and impress on G. R. Haywood, who was about to visit India as the representative of the Lancashire cotton interests, that the Government was their best friend and both able and willing to further their aims.[16] Wood, in other words, was trying to adopt and to justify a middle course in which Government would take only indirect action to stimulate cotton cultivation in India. He knew it would be difficult to explain this to Lancashire interests determined on more vigorous policies.

The difficulties of such tactics were at once revealed. Before leaving for India, Haywood wrote a letter to the Calcutta agents of the Cotton Supply

[14]Where there was no telegraph, horse expresses carried the information back and forth after the arrival of every English mail in Bombay. Frere to Wood, 26 Aug. 1862, no. 1 (encl.). Halifax Collection, India Office, Correspondence, India.

[15]Secretary of State to Government of India, Despatch no. 20 (Revenue), 25 July 1861.

[16]Wood to Clerk, 18 July 1861. Halifax Collection, I. O., Letter Books, VIII, p. 124. Haywood went to India in a dual capacity: as the agent of the Manchester Cotton Company, formed as a commercial venture in 1861 to purchase cotton in India and elsewhere; and as the secretary of the Cotton Supply Association.

Association setting out the policies Lancashire wished to see implemented in order to create conditions favourable to an improved supply of Indian cotton. These included the establishment of efficient courts in every cotton district, with power to enforce contracts between growers and purchasers of cotton; reduction of the stamp tax levied on all contracts; and changes in the "unsound and oppressive system of land tenure."[17] When Haywood's letter was referred to the Government of India it responded with indignation. It claimed great progress had been made in the improvement of local courts, denied that the stamp tax checked the investment of capital, and stated that the question of land tenures was under consideration.[18] But the agents of the Cotton Supply Association, while admitting that their complaint about the operation of the stamp tax was misinformed, repeated the complaints about the system of land tenures and again demanded modifications. The Government had implied that the Association was ignorant on the subject of land tenures and that the modifications they sought would infringe upon existing rights. These implications they rejected with the pious statement that "the Manchester Cotton Supply Association as a body of honorable Christian Gentlemen associated for a great national object" did not deserve the imputation of seeking to secure modifications in the system of land tenures in a way that would override established rights, or violate the principles of equity and justice "towards their fellow native subjects."[19]

Canning, the Governor-General of India, was alarmed at Lancashire's attitude, especially as it affected the question of land tenures. He detected in the tone of the Association's correspondence the first symptoms of a demand – arising from fear of a serious and prolonged shortage of cotton – for dangerously sweeping changes in the institutions of India while the country was still settling down after the Mutiny. The agent of the Association told him privately that what his employers were prepared to contend for was that the *ryots* (cultivators) should be compelled to change their condition of pauper occupiers of the soil to that of well-paid labourers, and that this should be done by law and under the active influence of government. Canning was worried that starvation and troubles in Lancashire would influence Parliament in the same direction. For this reason he was ready to do all that he thought could reasonably be expected

17Haywood to Messrs. Mosley and Hurst, 15 May 1861. Supplement to the *Calcutta Gazette,* LXXI, no. 49, 3 July 1861. See also Arthur Redford, *Manchester Merchants and Foreign Trade,* 2 vols. (Manchester, 1934 and 1956), esp. II, pp. 12–20.
18Government of India to Messrs. Mosley and Hurst, 2 July 1861. Supplement to the *Calcutta Gazette,* LXXI, no. 49, 3 July 1861. This rebuff received full support from the India Office; see Secretary of State to Government of India, Despatch no. 25 (Revenue), 8 Oct. 1861.
19Messrs. Mosley and Hurst to Government of India, 27 July 1861. Supplement to the *Calcutta Gazette,* LXXI, No. 74, 11 Dec. 1861.

on behalf of cotton before a clamour arose. In particular, he hoped that new orders regarding the sale of waste lands and redemption of the land revenue, currently being prepared by the Government of India, would cut the ground from under the Manchester malcontents and prevent any hasty move in Parliament.[20]

Wood, too, was worried. As a convinced free trader, he was opposed to all but a limited role for government in stimulating cotton production, and he was greatly concerned over the state of India's finances. But he was equally aware of the political dangers of not doing something to meet Lancashire's demands. Late in the summer of 1861 he warned Canning that there was great apprehension in Lancashire about future cotton supplies. Even if peace were concluded immediately, America could not have grown enough cotton in the current year to meet the demand, and there was every likelihood that the quantity grown would be diminished for the future. Wood hoped that this situation would stimulate cotton cultivation in India, since any fall in employment in the manufacturing districts would be a calamity. To escape criticism the Government would have to be able to show what action it had taken.[21] But Wood considered that the cotton interests should do more to help themselves. Towards the end of 1861 he remarked in exasperation that "the cotton people try my temper sadly. They have no regard for anything but their own selfish interest."[22] Nor was Wood alone in criticizing the attitude of the Lancashire cotton lobby. For example, A. C. Brice, a Bombay merchant with Manchester connections whose firm had established an agency in the Dharwar district of Bombay as early as 1854, observed in a letter to the *Daily News*:

> It is a remarkable fact that though the Manchester interest has been constantly urging on government the duty of their developing the resources of the country, it has nevertheless entirely withheld its pecuniary support from the railway undertakings which were the first and most important step towards effecting this object.[23]

The Calcutta newspaper, *The Englishman*, tartly observed: "Manchester will neither offer a fair or remunerative price; nor will she make the advances requisite to induce cultivation. Abjuring all risk herself, she calls on others to undertake for her what she is unwilling to embark on."[24] The *Edinburgh Review*, no friend to the Government of India, was equally critical of Lancashire. It pointed out that in the publications, reports, and

[20]Canning to Wood, 2 Sept. 1861. Halifax Collection, I. O., Corresp., India.
[21]Wood to Canning, 6 Aug. 1861. Halifax Collection, I. O., Letter Books, VIII, p. 176.
[22]Ibid., 26 Nov. 1861, IX, p. 125.
[23]Canning Papers, 114 (Papers on Miscellaneous Subjects), no. 805, *Daily News*, 10 May 1861.
[24]Ibid., 114, no. 777, *The Englishman*, 17 Oct. 1861.

correspondence of the past thirty years there was but one cry on the part of the cotton merchants and manufacturers – that government should do for them what they ought to have done for themselves.[25]

Wood's cautious approach to the cotton supply question was due not only to his free trade views and his concern for India's financial condition, but also to his knowledge of Lancashire's reservations about India as a permanent source of raw cotton. In October 1861 he was warned by a cotton spinner that if the American troubles ended and American cotton exports were resumed, it was likely that the cheaper American cotton would capture the market again.[26] For this reason Wood was unwilling to go too far to encourage the growth of cotton in India.[27] At the end of the year an event occurred to justify his caution. This was the *Trent* affair, which nearly brought about a conflict between Great Britain and the United States. This incident created what the Cotton Supply Association's publication, the *Cotton Supply Reporter*, called a "profound sensation" in the British cotton market. It was assumed in Lancashire that if war broke out between Great Britain and the United States, the North would have to lift the blockade of the Gulf ports. There was an immediate drop of 2d per lb. in the price of cotton on the Liverpool exchange, and even at this reduction only 4,000 bales were sold in two days. The *Cotton Supply Reporter* commented: "Fear of the American crop, by reducing prices, must remove a powerful stimulus to efforts which are being made in India and elsewhere to liberate us from dependence on one source of supply, and thus lessen our next week's receipts of raw material."[28]

Additional evidence that Lancashire was not really interested in buying large quantities of cotton from India at this time is provided by G. R. Haywood. Late in 1861, during his visit to India on behalf of the Manchester Cotton Company, he wrote to the chairman of the Company expressing regret that the directors had not sent out orders for the purchase of cotton.[29] In nearly every town and village he had passed through, growers had offered to sell him cotton, and Haywood feared that his failure to purchase would have a damaging effect on the Company's influence in the ensuing year.[30]

Haywood was optimistic about the possibilities of an Indian cotton

[25]*Edinburgh Review*, CVX (1862), p. 486.
[26]Wood to Canning, 18 Oct. 1861. Halifax Collection, I. O., Letter Books, IX, p. 28.
[27]Wood to Sir William Denison (Governor of Madras), 25 Oct. 1861. Halifax Collection, I. O., Letter Books, IX, p. 58.
[28]*Cotton Supply Reporter*, 16 Dec. 1861.
[29]Haywood was accompanied on his journey by Dr. G. F. Forbes, the superintendent of the government cotton gin factory at Dharwar. His services were placed at Haywood's disposal by the Secretary of State.
[30]Haywood to John Platt, 30 Nov. 1861. I.O., Rev. Dept., Home Corresp., Letters Received, IV, no. 264.

supply, particularly from the Dharwar district where American cotton had been acclimatized, but his optimism was not generally shared by merchants engaged in the cotton trade, in India or in England. Walter Cassels, one of the leading merchants of Bombay whose firm represented the Cotton Supply Association there, saw no reason to suppose that the exceptional demand for Indian cotton created by the American Civil War would survive that conflict. India's soil and climate were unsuitable and the quality of the Indian staple was poor. India could not therefore supply cotton of a quality suitable for the manufacture of fine cotton goods and so was unlikely to replace the United States as Lancashire's major source of cotton.[31] A similar conclusion was reached by Samuel Smith, a Liverpool cotton broker who visited India in 1863 at the request of the Manchester Chamber of Commerce. Smith summed up his impressions of India as a source of cotton for Lancashire in a series of letters to the *Bombay Times*. Smith also stressed the deficiencies of India's soil and climate and the inferior quality of India cotton as the limiting factors. He maintained that there was little hope of improvement in the methods of cotton cultivation in India for years to come, so that increased yield could not be looked for. Moreover, the cost of growing cotton in India in relation to other articles of produce was much greater than in America. Smith's conclusion was that India could never be a substitute for America though she could be a valuable supplement.[32]

The poor quality of Indian cotton led to difficulties which made many Lancashire manufacturers reluctant to use Indian cotton. For example, certain mills had become known as sellers of a uniform quality of yarn or cloth, and they did not find it to their advantage to introduce a new product which they might have to abandon if the supply of raw material failed, which was always possible under India's climatic conditions. Another impediment to the use of Indian cotton was the necessity to adapt spinning machinery for the short staple. Finally, the operatives did not like it. Short staple cotton required closer attention in spinning and at equal rates did not yield them equal wages.[33]

Such considerations reinforced the Government's caution in approaching the cotton supply question and confirmed its adherence to the limited policy laid down in the Resolution of 28 February 1861. Execution of that policy was left to the local governments. In July 1861 the Government of

[31]Walter R. Cassels, *Cotton: An Account of its Culture in Bombay Presidency* (Bombay, 1862), pp. 346–47. This work was one of the cotton handbooks commissioned by the Government of India. See p. 46, *n.* 40.

[32]*Bombay Times*, 12 Apr. 1863, encl. in Trevelyan to Wood, 2 May 1863. Halifax Collection, I. O., Corresp., India. Smith's articles were later published as a pamphlet: Samuel Smith, *The Cotton Trade of India* (London, 1863).

[33]Canning Papers, 114, no. 805, *Daily News*, 10 May 1861.

India went a step further and promised financial assistance to well-considered plans for improving roads likely to be of use in extending the cultivation of, or trade in, cotton if such projects could not be carried out from local resources or from imperial funds allocated in the current fiscal year.[34] It provided this assistance from funds held in reserve for public works. These were quickly used up and in October, despite its serious financial position, it announced additional grants, not exceeding twelve lakhs (£120,000), for the expansion of facilities for the export trade of India, especially the cotton export trade.[35]

In addition to these limited measures for the improvement of communications, the Government of India took three other steps in the first year of the American Civil War to encourage the production of cotton in India and improve its quality. The first was to offer prizes of Rs 10,000 in each of the three presidencies for the production of cotton of improved quality during the growing season 1861–62.[36] The India Office received notice of this decision without enthusiasm, the Secretary of State remarking that he expected little success from it when the stronger stimulus of private interest had failed to induce the cultivator to grow cotton of improved quality.[37] Events bore out this pessimism. For example, in Madras presidency there were only two competitors for the prize offered in 1861–62 and the cotton of one of them (an Indian) was so inferior that the competition was nominal. The whole prize of Rs 10,000 was awarded to a European firm.[38] In the following year, despite the offer of nine smaller prizes in place of one large prize and a decrease in the minimum extent of land to be cultivated to only ten acres, there was only one competitor – the previous year's winner. After this, it was decided that no further prizes would be offered.[39]

A second step taken by the Government of India was to order the compilation of special cotton handbooks from the public records of each presidency. The object was to describe measures taken in the past to increase the supply of Indian cotton to England and to improve its

[34]Resolution of the Governor-General in Council, no. 1806, 26 July 1861. India, Revenue Proceedings, XLVI, 26 July 1861, no. 19.

[35]Excerpt from a Circular issued in October 1861 by the Public Works Dept. of the Government of India and cited in "Public Works for the Purpose of Facilitating the Transit of Cotton to Ports of Shipment: A Memorandum by the Public Works Dept., Fort William, 5 June 1863," encl. in Trevelyan to Wood, 7 June 1863, no. 1. Halifax Collection, I. O., Corresp., India.

[36]Resolution of the Governor-General in Council, 9 Aug. 1861, encl. in Government of India to Secretary of State, Letter no. 13 (Revenue), 13 Aug. 1861.

[37]Secretary of State to Government of India, Despatch no. 30 (Revenue), 3 Dec. 1861.

[38]Madras Chamber of Commerce to Government of Madras, 31 July 1862. India, Rev. Procs., XLVII, 15 Sept. 1862, no. 2.

[39]Order no. 1767 of the Government of Madras, 25 Sept. 1863. India, Rev. Procs., XLVIII, 21 Oct. 1863, no. 31.

quality.[40] Handbooks were duly compiled for Bengal, Madras, and Bombay. They contain a good deal of information that is useful to the historian. It is hard to see what practical value they had at the time, except to acquit the authorities in India of past or present indifference to the cotton supply ·question.

A third measure was the provision by the Government of cotton-cleaning machinery. A cotton gin factory had been established by the Bombay government at Dharwar as part of the cotton improvement program undertaken by the East India Company in the 1840s. In 1854 it came under the superintendence of Dr. G. F. Forbes, a surgeon in the Bombay Army. Under his direction, the output of gins increased and the factory became a training school for young Indians in the repair and maintenance of gins supplied to the ryots from the main factory. By 1860 over 600 saw gins were in use in the Dharwar district.[41] In that year Forbes was sent to England to purchase cotton-cleaning machinery constructed there under his own supervision. After his return to India in the company of G. R. Haywood, the India Office on several occasions authorized expenditure of public funds for the manufacture in England of parts for new saw gins to be assembled at Dharwar.[42] The costs so incurred were recovered by the sale of the gins to the ryots. In the middle of 1862 Forbes reported that the rise in the price of cotton caused by the war in America had led to an increased demand for cotton-cleaning machinery, and that he had 591 registered applicants for gins who had paid a deposit against purchase of them when they became available. He also claimed that in the six years from 1856 to 1862 receipts from the sale of gins by the Government factory had fallen short of expenditure by only Rs 1,280.[43]

It is clear that during the first year of the American Civil War the attitude of the Government of India, supported by the Secretary of State, was one of extreme caution in undertaking measures to stimulate cotton production in India. It is equally clear that the reasons lay in the general failure of the cotton improvement program undertaken by the East India Company in the two preceding decades; the possibility in the earlier part of the war that supplies of cotton from the Southern states might still

[40]Resolution of the Governor-General in Council, 22 July 1861. India Office, Collections to Despatches (Revenue) to India, IX, no. 25.

[41]"Report on the Cotton Gin Factory in the Dharwar Collectorate for the Half Year ending 31 May 1862," *Selections from the Records of the Bombay Government,* new series, LXVII, p. 23; Haywood to Platt, 30 Nov. 1861. I. O., Rev. Dept., Home Corresp., Letters Rec., IV, no. 264; Cassels, op. cit., pp. 151–56.

[42]Under-Secretary of State to Dr. G. F. Forbes, 18 Jan. 1861; to J. M. Dunlop (manufacturer of cotton gins, Manchester), 24 Dec. 1861; and to secretary, Cotton Supply Association, 9 Jan. and 22 Mar. 1862. I. O., Rev. Dept., Home Corresp., Letters Sent, I, nos. 66, 113, 114, 118, and 134.

[43]"Report on the Cotton Gin Factory . . . for the Half Year ending 31 May 1862." *Selections from the Records of the Bombay Government,* n. s., LXVII, p. 21.

become available to Lancashire; and the belief that once the troubles in America ended, Lancashire would resume her former dependence on that country for supplies of raw cotton. Underlying these factors was the firm adherence of the Secretary of State to the principles of *laissez-farie*. Government policy in 1861–62 was accordingly restricted to a very limited program of public works designed to expedite the transport of cotton from the interior to ports of export, and to such other measures as might indirectly aid the cultivation of cotton without involving the Government in a role that it considered better left to private enterprise.

In 1862, as cotton imports into Great Britain declined, the Government came under increasing pressure to take more vigorous action to ensure larger supplies of Indian cotton (see Table 3.1). In the spring, Henry Dunlop, the chairman of the Glasgow Chamber of Commerce, wrote to the Governor-General, Lord Elgin, telling him that the prospects of a supply of cotton from America were getting worse every day. India was the only practicable alternative source and he urged the Government of India to take even extraordinary measures to promote both increased cultivation of cotton and improvement in its quality. He suggested that it would be useful to disperse over the cotton-growing areas fifty officers from regiments then being disbanded to convey "useful intelligence" to the ryots.[44] Elgin agreed that great interests were at stake, affecting India even more than Great Britain, and he was not so strongly wedded to the dogmas of political economy as to be unwilling to use government agency to promote an economic end such as the improvement of cotton cultivation. But he believed that abnormal interference by government might check the natural operation of the laws of supply and demand on capitalists and cultivators alike.[45]

In July, the Manchester Chamber of Commerce drew up a memorandum justifying government intervention to stimulate cotton production in India. It began by paying lip service to the "ordinary laws of supply and demand" in solving the problem of cotton supply, and said that the interruption or even the total destruction of the American supply did not justify any departure from the recognized principles of free trade. But it then went on to argue that proposals which had been made for government intervention to ensure new supplies from India stood on different ground. The construction of public works such as roads and canals would be of great advantage to India whether or not they were remunerative as separate enterprises. Such public works were of a permanent nature and did not depend for their success on the future failure of the American cotton supply. They were comparatively free from the serious risk of loss which

[44]Dunlop to Elgin, 24 Mar. 1862. Elgin Papers, Letters from Miscellaneous, pp. 9–13.
[45]Elgin to Dunlop, 21 May 1862. Elgin Papers, Letters to Miscellaneous, pp. 12–28.

had hitherto deterred private speculators from attempting to increase the production of cotton in India, namely, the risk of failure due to resumption of supplies of American cotton. This was the Chamber's reply "to the charge that the manufacturers of this district have been wilfully blind to their own interest and the public good, in hesitating to engage themselves either individually or collectively, in attempting to provide an adequate supply of cotton."[46] The memorandum ended with a categorical rejection of the idea that the Manchester merchants should enter into a new and extended business for the purpose of providing the raw material.

In face of this attitude, the authorities felt no responsibility for undertaking what private enterprise itself was unwilling to do. Elgin expressed the Government of India's view in September 1862 when he admitted that India undoubtedly had a service to render England and the world in the matter of cotton supply, while criticizing the "preposterous character of the proposals for effecting this object made to us by persons who used to enjoy a reputation for commonsense and fairness."[47] One such proposal mentioned by Elgin was the suggestion that the Government of India should buy up all the cotton in the country and transport it to the coast on the chance of its finding a market there. John Bright proposed that the Government should exempt from tax all land on which cotton was grown. This prompted Sir Charles Wood to exclaim caustically: "It certainly is amusing to see how totally forgetful of their principles the Manchester people are, where their own interests are concerned. They would give bounty or protection or anything else."[48] Wood told the Governor of Bombay that he was tired of the never-ceasing applications for outlay by the Government from parties who would do nothing to help themselves. "I do not believe that those who want cotton here will in reality stir a finger. They will complain, and ask for expenditures, on the chance of good accruing to themselves, but they will do nothing."[49]

Were Wood's charges justified? The evidence shows that after the outbreak of war in America a number of companies were formed in England to obtain supplies of cotton from India.[50] The most important of these was the Manchester Cotton Company, but Lancashire's reluctance to look to India as a permanent source of supply had a dampening effect on its efforts.[51] The company struggled on for more than three years before

---

[46]*Proceedings of the Manchester Chamber of Commerce*, 16 July 1862.
[47]Elgin to Samuel Laing, 9 Sept. 1862. Elgin Papers, Letters to Miscellaneous, pp. 54–55.
[48]Wood to Trevelyan, 22 Dec. 1862. Halifax Collection, I. O., Letter Books, XI, p. 352. In the previous year Wood had been asked to send a member of his Council to India to purchase cotton.
[49]Wood to Frere, 29 Aug. 1862. Halifax Collection, I. O., Letter Books, XI, p. 104.
[50]Henderson, op. cit., p. 40.
[51]The activities of the Manchester Cotton Company in India are described in ch. 4.

going into liquidation in 1864; and the other companies formed in this period had no better success.[52]

Despite such failures, large quantities of Indian cotton were reaching England by 1862, as the figures in Table 3.1 show. Nevertheless, as the war in America entered its third year, Lancashire renewed its demands

Table 3.1

Quantities of Raw Cotton Imported into Great Britain from India, and Total Cotton Imports, 1855–72

Year	Imports of Cotton from India (lb.)	Total Cotton Imports (lb.)	Imports from India as per cent of Total Imports
1855	145,179,216	891,751,052	16
1856	180,496,624	1,023,886,394	18
1857	250,338,144	969,318,896	26
1858	132,722,576	1,034,342,176	13
1859	192,330,880	1,225,989,072	16
1860	204,141,168	1,390,938,758	15
1861	369,040,448	1,256,984,736	29
1862	392,654,528	523,973,296	75
1863	434,420,784	669,583,264	65
1864	506,527,392	893,304,720	56
1865	445,947,600	977,978,288	45
1866	615,302,240	1,377,128,936	45
1867	496,317,008	1,262,536,912	39
1868	493,706,640	1,328,084,016	37
1869	481,377,344	1,220,309,856	39
1870	341,536,008	1,339,367,120	26
1871	431,209,744	1,778,189,776	24
1872	443,234,736	1,408,837,472	31

SOURCES: *Statistical Abstract for the United Kingdom in Each of the Last Fifteen Years from 1855 to 1869*, in *Parliamentary Papers*, LXVIII (1870), C. 145, Table 18; *Statistical Abstract . . . from 1858 to 1872*, ibid., LXIX (1873), C. 833, Table 20.

for increased government activity to stimulate cotton production in India. In May 1863 Wood was asked to supply the ryots with American seed; he also received a request, which he thought impossible but passed on to the Governor of Bombay, Sir Bartle Frere, that "some sort of apostles be sent around the country to indoctrinate the ryots and spread the elements of sound agriculture."[53] Frere believed that government action would be useful in extending and improving cotton cultivation provided that too great and too immediate results were not

[52]See Henderson, op. cit., 129–31 for statistics on the formation of limited liability companies between 1856 and 1865, their duration, and their mode of dropping out.

[53]Wood to Frere, 4 May 1863. Halifax Collection, I. O., Letter Books, XIII, pp. 34–35.

expected, if it was accepted that there would be numerous failures, and if a liberal discretion were given to government officials entrusted with the task. He did not think that the Government could do much to increase the quantity of cotton produced, since that would be determined by price. But he thought the Government could do much to improve quality by various means, such as promoting the growth of better varieties, the use of superior agricultural techniques, and the use of better appliances to clean and pack the cotton. In particular, he recommended that the superintendent of the gin factory at Dharwar, G. F. Forbes, should be given a wider sphere of operations and that similarly qualified men should be employed in other cotton districts.[54]

In making these proposals, Frere expressed a viewpoint close to that of the Lancashire manufacturers who demanded government intervention to bring about India's economic development:

> I would not have suggested this two years ago, when it might have been reasonably expected that private enterprize [sic] would have done all that was wanted. But I see no signs of their coming forward in time to be of use in the present crisis. The laws which make such private skill and enterprize so potent elsewhere, no doubt operate here as in America or England; but what with distance, adverse interests, and adverse agencies of various kinds, the strength of the law is so weakened and slow in action, that it is practically inoperative, and while I cannot interfere, and supersede the natural law, I think the case is one where government interference may be excused, and looking to the great national objects to be arrived at, may be more than justified.[55]

The political climate in England made Wood receptive to Frere's suggestions. He had been under heavy attack from Lancashire since the latter part of 1862 and there had even been talk of impeaching him.[56] Nothing materialized when the new session of Parliament opened in February 1863 and he was able to tell Lord Elgin that "not an adverse whisper was heard."[57] But in May he came under attack for drastically modifying the new rules of sale for waste lands in India and for vetoing the Government of India's proposals for the redemption of the land revenue. He was then accused of having done nothing since assuming office in 1859 to encourage the growth of cotton in India or to improve its quality.[58] Wood rode out this storm only to face another in July, when a motion was presented in the House of Commons calling for the appointment

[54]Frere to Wood, 6 June 1863. Halifax Collection, I. O., Corresp., India.
[55]Ibid.
[56]Wood to Elgin, 9 Oct. 1862. Halifax Collection, I. O., Letter Books, XI, p. 80.
[57]Ibid., 10 Feb. 1863, XII, p. 72.
[58]Great Britain, *Parliamentary Debates*, 3rd series, vol. CLXX, cols. 1622 and 1645–46, 12 May 1863.

of a Select Committee to enquire whether any further measures could legitimately be taken by the Government of India in order to increase the supply of cotton from India.[59] In the ensuing debate, the chief pillar of the Manchester School, Richard Cobden, referred to taunts that the Lancashire interests did not maintain their principles of free trade when dealing with Indian questions. He suggested, as had the Governor of Bombay, that the principles of Adam Smith did not govern relations between Great Britain and India and he argued that the national calamity which the interruption of cotton supplies from America had brought about justified intervention by the Government.[60] Wood defended himself in a lengthy speech, in which he chided his opponents for departing from the principles of free trade:

> My conviction is, that an adequate demand, evidenced by a rise in price, will produce an adequate supply. I have held those political principles throughout all my political life with the greatest confidence, and on former occasions they were warmly advocated by gentlemen who belong to what is called the Manchester School, and who declared that the best and kindest thing that could be done for trade and manufactures was to leave them alone, and that bounties and protection were not only hurtful to the community at large, but to the very trade itself which was protected.[61]

Wood stated that the Government of India was perfectly prepared to take any measures within the bounds of its legitimate functions to promote cotton cultivation but he challenged his critics to state precisely what they thought ought to be done. He admitted that the Government of India had one imperative duty: the improvement of communications. But he rejected any proposal for large-scale cultivation of cotton by the Government or for the purchase of cotton by the Government.

Wood was pleased with his speech and believed that he would hear no more of the charges levelled against him.[62] He had reiterated the position he had adopted from the first: that the role of government in stimulating cotton cultivation in India must be a strictly limited one, despite distressed conditions in Lancashire. Subject to this principle, he was prepared to sanction measures such as those proposed by the Governor of Bombay for the improvement of the quality of Indian cotton.

In sanctioning such measures, Wood did not abandon his adherence to *laissez-faire*. For example, he was prepared to authorize the Government of Bombay to extend the sphere of Forbes's usefulness as superintendent of the Government gin factory, either by increasing the means at his

[59]Ibid., CLXXII, col. 178, 3 July 1863.
[60]Ibid., cols. 199–201, 3 July 1863.
[61]Ibid., cols. 209–22, 3 July 1863.
[62]Wood to Trevelyan, 10 July 1863. Halifax Collection, I. O., Letter Books, XIII, p. 152.

command to supply machinery, or by selecting one or two officers to do in different areas what Forbes was doing in Dharwar. But further than this he would not go. "To this extent I am willing that the Government should lend its aid to encourage the growth and preparation for the market of the best description of cotton; but I am persuaded that any interference, direct or indirect, on the part of the public servants, with the free agency of the ryots, would be productive of more harm than good."[63] In keeping with these instructions, Dr. Forbes was appointed Cotton Commissioner for Bombay with the tasks of improving the machinery for cleaning indigenous cotton, superintending the supply of acclimatized American seed from Dharwar to persons wishing to extend exotic cotton cultivation elsewhere, and generally assuming responsibility for problems connected with the improvement and extension of cotton cultivation in Bombay.[64] The Government of India, in commenting on these instructions, cautiously reminded the Bombay government of the "importance and soundness" of the principle laid down by the Secretary of State that any direct or indirect interference on the part of public servants with the free agency of the ryots would produce more harm than good.[65] In other words, the duties of Forbes as Cotton Commissioner were to be limited to advice and assistance. This was made plain to the Cotton Supply Association when it proposed in October 1863 that Commissioners should be appointed for each of three areas of India where they considered the soil and climate favourable to the cultivation of exotic cotton, and that such Commissioners should act as Joint Collectors with the power to issue orders to subordinate Indian officials.[66] The India Office tartly rejected this proposal which, it said, would bring the direct authority of government to bear on agriculture and commerce in India.[67] It did, however, sanction the appointment of a Superintendent of Cotton Affairs in Wardha district, an important cotton-growing area in the Central Provinces and subsequently it created the post of Cotton Commissioner for the Central Provinces and Berar.

Such caution did not satisfy Lancashire. In March 1865, as the American Civil War was drawing to a close, the Cotton Supply Association sent a

[63]Secretary of State to Government of Bombay, Despatch no. 26 (Revenue), 17 July 1863.

[64]Government of Bombay to Secretary of State, Letter no. 17 (Revenue), 27 Aug. 1863, submitting copy of Bombay Government Resolution appointing Dr. Forbes as Cotton Commissioner subject to the approval of the Secretary of State. Forbes was appointed on 1 Oct. 1863.

[65]Government of India to Government of Bombay, no. 6033, 17 Oct. 1863. India, Rev. Procs., XLVIII, 17 Oct. 1863, no. 15.

[66]"Minute for the Secretary of State in reference to the appointment of Commissioners in India for the cultivation of a better quality cotton, as suggested in an interview held lately between the Secretary of State and Messrs. Cheetham and Ashworth," dated 19 Aug. 1863. I. O., Rev. Dept., Home Corresp., Letters Rec., V, no. 443.

[67]Under-Secretary of State to John Cheetham and Edmund Ashworth, 30 Oct. 1863. I. O., Rev. Dept., Home Corresp., Letters Sent, II, no. 223.

memorial to the Secretary of State expressing deep regret that, despite the stimulus provided by a period of scarcity, so little had been done to improve the quality of Indian cotton. Even at that late stage it asked that further measures be taken.[68] Wood responded with a review of what had been done and argued that if the great increase in the price of Indian cotton did not offer sufficient inducement to the ryots to increase the extent of cotton cultivation, nothing the Government could do would be of any use. "It must now be obvious to everyone that the high prices for cotton have afforded an adequate stimulus to an increased production in India almost beyond what had been desirable for the benefit of the inhabitants of that country."[69]

The statistical evidence supports Wood's contention. Figures in Table 3.2 show the extent to which cotton cultivation expanded in the principal cotton-growing regions of British India in the 1860s. These figures show that the American war, by raising the price of cotton, stimulated a general increase in the amount of land under cotton cultivation. At the same time a rise in the retail price of food grains took place which apparently raised the spectre of famine in Wood's mind. In April 1864 his old colleague of Irish famine days, Sir Charles Trevelyan, whom he had appointed Finance Member of the Governor-General's Council in 1862, went so far as to compare conditions in Bombay presidency with those which had prevailed in Ireland in 1846–47.[70] This was a great exaggeration, but such alarmism from a trusted friend holding high office in India helps explain Wood's mistaken belief that cotton cultivation had reached its safe limit by 1865.[71]

In rebuffing Lancashire, Wood could also point to the volume of British imports of Indian raw cotton. These continued to rise after 1862, although India's share of total British imports of cotton declined from then on (see Table 3.1). After 1866, however, the flood of cotton from India slackened and though imports from that country remained above the

[68] Memorial of the Cotton Supply Association, 28 Mar. 1865. I. O., Rev. Dept., Home Corresp., Letters Rec., VII, no. 588.

[69] Assistant Under-Secretary of State to J. Cheetham, 11 Apr. 1865. I. O., Rev. Dept., Home Corresp., Letters Sent, III, no. 315.

[70] India, *Legislative Council Proceedings*, n.s., III (1864), p. 147. Trevelyan's statement provoked an indignant rejoinder from the Governor of Bombay. See Frere to Wood, 28 April 1864, I. O., Corresp., India. Sir Richard Temple, who was Chief Commissioner of the Central Provinces for most of the period 1862–65 later wrote: "In some places, despite good harvests, food grains were sold so dear as to amount to famine prices, yet the people seemed to thrive, doubtless because of their prosperity in other ways. The peasant proprietors were foremost in the race of temporary prosperity. They engaged largely in the cotton carrying business, employing their carts and bullocks for that purpose. They gained good wages on the public works at every season when they were not busy in their fields." Sir Richard Temple, *Men and Events of My Time in India* (London: John Murray, 1882), p. 269.

[71] For the growth of cotton cultivation in India in the period 1861–70 in relation to the cultivation of cereal crops, see Peter Harnetty, "Cotton Exports and Indian Agriculture, 1861–70," *Economic History Review*, 2nd series, XXIV (1971), pp. 414–29.

Table 3.2

Cultivation of cotton in major cotton-producing provinces of British India, 1860–61 to 1869–70,
(in acres)
with indexes of absolute increases over 1860–61
(1860–61 = 100)

Year	Bombay		Central Provinces		Berar		North-Western Provinces		Madras		Punjab		Total	
1860–61	1,002,196	100	358,000	100	620,000	100	950,000	100	1,060,558	100	467,513	100	4,458,267	100
1861–62	1,140,434	114	375,623	104	650,000	104	953,076	100	1,020,184	96	481,351	102	4,620,668	104
1862–63	1,309,484	130	427,111	119	753,571	122	985,578	104	1,309,234	123	547,414	117	5,332,392	120
1863–64	1,517,321	151	588,436	164	1,137,833	184	1,135,688	120	1,766,312	167	537,183	114	6,682,773	150
1864–65	1,573,447	156	691,198	193	1,196,300	192	1,730,634	182	1,747,501	164	872,851	186	7,811,931	175
1865–66	1,186,097	118	587,398	164	910,310	146	885,102	93	1,395,697	132	613,262	131	5,578,176	125
1866–67	1,435,183	143	598,801	167	1,238,966	200	1,112,677	117	1,316,944	124	624,193	134	6,326,764	142
1867–68	1,436,735	143	644,271	180	1,254,522	202	987,727	104	1,486,861	140	687,321	147	6,497,437	146
1868–69	1,436,613	143	671,336	188	1,286,742	208	891,444	94	1,341,365	126	679,294	145	6,306,734	141
1869–70	1,978,711	197	669,593	187	1,415,786	228	1,118,560	118	1,604,028	151	835,053	178	7,621,731	171

SOURCES: For Bombay, Resolution No. 6092 of the Government of Bombay, 27 October 1875. Bombay, Revenue (Lands) Procs., vol. 466 (1875); for Madras, Revenue Dept. Procs., 5 November 1870. no. 80; for the other provinces, *Annual Administration Reports and Reports on the Administration of the Land Revenue.*

pre-war figure, India's share of the British market declined and this, combined with the parallel increase in imports of cotton from America, alarmed those in Lancashire who did not wish to see Great Britain returning to her former dependence on American cotton. The Cotton Supply Association accordingly returned to the attack once more and in 1869 it again urged on the India Office the desirability of experimental cultivation of cotton in India, as well as irrigation works, road building, railway construction, and the improvement of inland waterways.[72]

The Vice-President of the Council of India at the time was H.T. Prinsep, who had been a director of the former East India Company. He proposed a strong reply to "those Manchester people" reminding them of how much the Government had done to promote cotton cultivation. Other members of the Council and the Secretary of State, the Duke of Argyll, agreed. But Argyll did not agree with the doctrine implied by Sir Charles Wood in his reply to the Association in 1865, that the ordinary laws of supply and demand could be trusted to produce speedily the most improved methods of growth or preparation of cotton for the market. He realized that new habits and ideas in respect to such matters made their way very slowly and that often one active and enterprising man could do in a few years work that might otherwise take generations. "The government has already gone too far, and done too much," declared Argyll, "to be able to take up the ground that we can or ought to leave cotton cultivation to take care of itself."[73] Accordingly, a comprehensive reply was drawn up in the India Office summarizing the steps that had been taken under government auspices to stimulate cotton cultivation in India since experiments had first been undertaken by the East India Company in the 1840s. These included expenditure, on experiments designed to improve cotton cultivation, of a sum computed at £187,000 by 1857; expenditure by 1869 of £20,000 a year in the form of salaries to officers whose sole duty was to superintend the experimental cultivation of cotton; the appointment of a Cotton Commissioner for Bombay in 1863 and for the Central Provinces in 1866; the enactment of Cotton Frauds legislation by the Bombay Legislative Council in 1863 and the consequent creation of a large inspecting establishment throughout the Bombay presidency; and the operation of a cotton gin factory at Dharwar which had supplied 2,000 gins since its inception and which also provided maintenance of gins located too far from the factory to be brought there for repair.[74]

This statement reveals the extent to which Government, despite its

[72]Memorial of the Cotton Supply Association, 12 Mar. 1869. I. O., Rev. Dept., Home Corresp., Letters Rec., X, no. 1191.
[73]Note by H. T. Prinsep, n.d., and Memorandum by the Duke of Argyll, 25 Mar. 1869. I. O., Rev. Dept., Home Corresp., Letters Sent, V, no. 612.
[74]Loc. cit.

obvious reluctance, became involved in the cotton supply question in the mid-nineteenth century. The Government's responses to the pressures exerted by Lancashire were determined by two main factors: first, the free trade views of Sir Charles Wood, expressed in his correspondence with officials in India and in statements of policy in Parliament, notably his speech in the House of Commons on 3 July 1863; second, the belief – for which there was much supporting evidence – that Lancashire would resume its former dependence on the United States as soon as supplies of cotton again became available from that source, leaving India with greatly expanded production and no markets. Lancashire, on the other hand, took the view that orthodox principles of *laissez-faire* did not apply to India, since that country was a special case in which conditions justified direct governmental intervention. To secure its object, Lancashire employed its well-tried political techniques and successfully forced the Government to intervene more than it wished in order to stimulate the supply of cotton to Great Britain.

Table 3.3

Quantities of Raw Cotton Exported from India, 1861–72

Year	Quantity (lb.)	Year	Quantity (lb.)
1861–62	392,700,000	1867–68	614,056,049
1862–63	473,678,421	1868–69	697,630,796
1863–64	550,126,402	1869–70	554,834,522
1864–65	525,052,876	1870–71	577,600,764
1865–66	893,150,424	1871–72	800,246,087
1866–67	425,568,892		

SOURCES: *Statistical Abstract Relating to British India, 1863–72*, in *Parliamentary Papers*, LXIX (1873), C. 870, Table 24 for the years 1862–63 to 1871–72. The figure for 1861–62 is taken from India, Dept. of Revenue and Agriculture, *Note on Indian Cotton* (Simla, 1888), p. 9. Earlier *Statistical Abstracts Relating to British India* do not give figures of quantities of cotton exports from India.

But Lancashire weakened its case by its eagerness to resume its dependence on America as its principal source of supply as soon as the cotton-producing states recovered from the effects of the Civil War. Exports of cotton from India, which had averaged only 225 million lb. a year in the decade 1850–60, had risen dramatically in the 1860s, as shown in Table 3.3.[75] Meanwhile, as the figures in Table 3.4 indicate, the

[75]Unlike British statistics for imports and exports, which were based on the calendar year, Indian statistics were based on the fiscal year. This ended on 30 April until 1866 and 31 March thereafter. This should be kept in mind in interpreting the statistics in Table 3.3 and in making comparisons with Table 3.1.

quantity of Indian cotton consumed in Great Britain declined while consumption of American cotton rose in the post-1865 period.[76]

Table 3.4
Consumption of Cotton in Great Britain, 1855–72
Average per week
(in bales)

Year	Total Consumption	U.S.A.		India	
		Quantity	Per cent of Total	Quantity	Per cent of Total
1855	40,403	30,278	74.9	5,383	13.3
1856	41,987	31,291	74.5	5,181	12.3
1857	39,065	27,111	69.4	7,079	18.1
1858	41,817	31,452	75.2	6,240	14.9
1859	44,167	36,625	82.9	3,504	7.9
1860	48,523	41,094	84.7	3,340	6.9
1861	45,454	34,782	76.5	6,702	14.7
1862	22,795	4,816	21.1	13,428	58.9
1863	26,492	2,264	8.5	17,169	64.8
1864	30,123	3,085	10.2	17,677	58.6
1865	39,129	5,078	12.9	20,743	53.0
1866	45,892	17,335	37.8	17,458	38.0
1867	49,471	20,605	41.6	17,426	35.2
1868	53,883	21,469	39.8	15,409	28.5
1869	50,547	17,844	35.3	18,055	35.7
1870	53,790	28,218	52.4	13,620	25.3
1871	59,899	34,790	58.1	10,306	17.2
1872	62,800	27,630	44.0	13,260	21.1

SOURCE: Thomas Ellison, *The Cotton Trade of Great Britain* (London: Effingham Wilson, 1886), Table 1.

As these figures show, India was able to maintain a high level of cotton exports despite the decline in British consumption of India cotton. This was so because the opening of the Suez Canal in 1869 and the development of steamships helped India develop new markets for her cotton in continental Europe and Japan. In addition there was a growing demand from the developing Indian mill industry.

In 1872, the Cotton Supply Association disbanded and this marks the end of any serious or sustained interest in India as a major source

[76]Even during the period of the so-called "cotton famine" in Lancashire, from 1861–65, a large proportion of the cotton imported into Great Britain from India was re-exported to continental European markets. This can be seen by comparing the percentage figures in Tables 3.1 and 3.4. For further evidence on this point see Eugene A. Brady, "A Reconsideration of the Lancashire 'Cotton Famine'," *Agricultural History*, XXXVII (1963), pp. 156–62. See also Frenise A. Logan, "India's Loss of the British Cotton Market after 1865," *Journal of Southern History*, XXXI (1965), pp. 40–50.

of Great Britain's raw cotton. The main legacies of the activities of Lancashire cotton manufacturers in developing India as a source of raw material were a public works program, in which many projects were undertaken solely with a view to expediting the export of cotton, and a cotton improvement program, designed to bring the quality of Indian cotton to a standard acceptable to Lancashire.

4

COTTON AND PUBLIC WORKS

"THE GREAT OBSTACLES to any increase in the supply or improvement in the quality of the cotton of central India, are the enormous expense, loss of time, deterioration from exposure . . . incurred by the present mode of transport," wrote the Glasgow Chamber of Commerce in 1847.[1] The need for a program of public works was an essential element in the argument of British cotton manufacturers that India should be developed to serve the interests of British industry. They had two objects in view: to increase the quantity and improve the quality of the cotton available from India. Lancashire's pressure on the government to secure an increase in the supply of cotton from India has been discussed in the previous chapter and subsequent chapters will examine measures taken by government in an attempt to improve the quality of Indian cotton. This chapter is concerned with projects undertaken in India in the mid-nineteenth century in response to demands from British textile interests for improvement in India's internal communications in order to facilitate the export of cotton.

The demands were stimulated by the "cotton famine" of 1846 which prompted John Bright, who represented Manchester in Parliament, to launch a campaign for the appointment of a parliamentary committee to

[1]Quoted by W. J. MacPherson, "Investment in Indian Railways, 1845–1875," *Economic History Review,* 2nd ser., VIII (1955), p. 184.

inquire into the question of cotton in India. Bright was successful in securing the appointment of a Select Committee, with himself as chairman, in February 1848 and much of its attention was devoted to the need for improved land transport to tap the cotton-growing areas of India.[2] Although Bright did not think that his committee's *Report* was of much value, the evidence published with it did serve as a principal source for the program of public works which the cotton interests urged on the Government of India during the next dozen years.[3]

A fresh opportunity for the expression of Lancashire's views on the subject of Indian development came in 1853 when the renewal of the East India Company's charter came before Parliament. Bright announced that he would oppose renewal because of the Company's neglect of public works, shown by the evidence submitted to his Select Committee five years earlier. With the assistance of other Lancashire members of Parliament, he formed the Indian Reform Society to oppose the necessary legislation in the House of Commons.[4] The debate on the bill revealed both the bitterness of the Lancashire group at what it considered the apathetic attitude of the East India Company in regard to public works and the readiness of the Government to provide the necessary spur for the development of India's communications. Bright and his supporters repeatedly attacked the Company for its failure to build roads, railways, and canals.[5] For the Government, the President of the Board of Control, Sir Charles Wood, freely admitted that railways and public works were important to the British cotton interests and promised that they would be built, to the extent that finances permitted, as soon as definite proposals were received from the Government of India.[6]

Wood's statement in Parliament did more than reflect the natural desire of a politican to appease a powerful pressure group, although he had a healthy respect for the power of the cotton lobby at a time when the position of Lord Aberdeen's coalition ministry was precarious.[7] His

---

[2]*Report from the Select Committee on the Growth of Cotton in India,* in *Parliamentary Papers* (1847–48), IX, No. 511; Daniel Thorner, *Investment in Empire: British Railway and Steam Shipping Enterprise in India, 1825–1849* (Philadelphia: University of Pennsylvania Press, 1950), p. 146.

[3]Arthur W. Silver, *Manchester Men and Indian Cotton, 1847–1872* (Manchester: Manchester University Press, 1966), p. 24.

[4]For a detailed analysis of Lancashire's influence on public works and railway policy at this time, see R. J. Moore, "Imperialism and 'Free Trade' Policy in India, 1853–4," *Econ. Hist. Rev.,* 2nd ser., XVII (1964), pp. 135–45.

[5]Great Britain, *Parliamentary Debates,* 3rd series, vol. CXXVII, cols. 1179–80 (Bright) and 1238 (Phillimore), 6 June 1853; ibid., CXXVIII, cols. 766 (Blackett), 823 (Cobden), 877–88 (Bright), and 1009–16 (Seymour), 24, 27, and 30 June 1853.

[6]Ibid., CXXVII, cols. 111–18, 3 June 1853.

[7]R. J. Moore, *Sir Charles Wood's Indian Policy, 1853–66* (Manchester: Manchester University Press, 1966), pp. 124–25.

private correspondence reveals that he was constantly exhorting the Governor-General of India, Lord Dalhousie, to push forward schemes for railways, roads, and irrigation projects. When Dalhousie's proposals eventually came before him, he gave his prompt consent, at the same time repeating his desire to open up communications between the great cotton-growing districts of the interior of India and the west coast.[8]

For a time, Wood's exertions won the grudging support of the Manchester School, due to "his attentiveness to the cotton question and from his vigorous prosecution of railways and public works."[9] But soon, dissatisfaction set in. Railway construction was slow and by April 1858, although £34,231,000 had been sanctioned for building railways, only 322 miles had actually been opened.[10] Moreover, in order to cope with the financial problems caused by the suppression of the Indian Rebellion, the Government of India placed an embargo on all but essential public works. This occurred at a time when the cotton interests, through the Manchester Chamber of Commerce and the Cotton Supply Association, were pressing for numerous projects – including canals, roads, harbours, and piers, as well as railways – designed to facilitate the transport and export of Indian cotton.[11] The Cotton Supply Association suggested a public loan of £20 million for opening up the river navigation of India and for the construction of roads, bridges, piers, docks, canals, and railways.[12] Lord Stanley, who became the first Secretary of State for India in September 1858, following the assumption of the Government of India by the Crown, favoured a scheme for local loans, whereby funds would be raised in a particular district for public works in that district, but the Government of India rejected this as unworkable.[13] Nor did the Government of India favour Lancashire's solution of a state loan for public works, mainly because it feared that it would be difficult to confine the proceeds of such a loan to such a purpose if another emergency such as the Rebellion arose.

[8]Wood to Dalhousie, 24 March, 8 April, and 30 July 1853. Halifax Collection, India Board, Letter Books, III, pp. 40, 52.

[9]Moore, "Imperialism and 'Free Trade' Policy in India, 1853–4," op. cit., p. 144.

[10]East India (Revenues), *Statement of the Extent of the Several Lines of Railway ... together with an Account of the Progress made, and of the Expense Incurred*, in *Parl. Papers* (1857–58), XLII, No. 201-VII. A parliamentary committee was set up in April 1858 to inquire into the delays that had occurred in railway construction in India and its Report, with evidence, is in ibid., XIV, No. 416.

[11]*Proceedings of the Manchester Chamber of Commerce* (Manchester Central Reference Library), vol. 5 (1849–58), 16 Apr. 1857; proposals of the Cotton Supply Association, encl. in Court of Directors to Government of India, Despatch no. 42 (Public Works), 14 Oct. 1857.

[12]*Cotton Supply Reporter*, 1 Oct. 1858.

[13]Secretary of State to Government of India, Despatch no. 12 (P.W.), 24 Mar. 1859; Government of India to Secretary of State, Letter no. 71 (P.W.), 19 Sept. 1860.

While the financial crisis caused by the Rebellion was holding back development projects in India, the mounting crisis in America was posing a serious threat to Lancashire's cotton supply. Consequently, in February 1861, the Manchester Chamber of Commerce proposed to Sir Charles Wood, who had succeeded Stanley as Secretary of State in June 1859, that the Government of India should raise a development loan of from £30 million to £40 million for internal public works. It emphasized the danger to Lancashire's cotton supply posed by the threat of war in America; noted that India could not emerge as a major source of raw cotton without good roads and effective means of transport; and stressed the Government's duty to carry out such works.[14]

The response to this proposal was not encouraging to the cotton interests. As already noted in chapter 3, Wood had just raised a loan of £3 million for railway construction and he was unwilling to add further to India's public debt in a period of financial crisis. In India, the Government was prepared to admit that the improvement of communications was within its legitimate functions and that it should do something to facilitate the anticipated increase in the export of cotton in 1861–62. But only limited measures were taken. They excluded railways, canals, and metalled roads, which were major projects requiring much money and time, and were restricted to the improvement of country cart and bullock tracks, works that could be done cheaply and would open up hitherto inaccessible areas of the country. The Government of India also promised limited financial aid for projects recommended by provincial governments which would help in extending the cultivation of, or trade in, cotton.[15] In fact, it found itself obliged to go somewhat further. It had allocated a sum only slightly exceeding £1 million for the improvement of communications in 1861–62; by the end of the year it had spent a further £600,000 for this purpose and was preparing to increase appropriations for the following year.[16]

In London, Wood found himself in a difficult position. On the one hand, he was concerned over the state of India's finances and, on the other, he feared that if Lancashire's cotton supplies petered out because of the American Civil War there would be widespread unemployment in the manufacturing districts. The onus would then be upon the government to show that it had done what it could to develop alternative sources of cotton.[17] Wood's problem was to act without compromising the *laissez-faire*

[14]*Proceedings of the Manchester Chamber of Commerce*, vol. 6 (1858–67), 27 Feb. 1861.

[15]Resolution of the Governor-General in Council, no. 1806, 26 July 1861, India, Revenue Proceedings, XLVI, 26 July 1861, no. 19.

[16]Government of India to Secretary of State, Letters no. 89 and no. 5 (P.W.), 23 Dec. 1861 and 28 Jan. 1862.

[17]Wood to Canning, 6 Aug. 1861. Halifax Collection, India Office, Letter Books, VIII, p. 176.

doctrine of a balanced budget. In June 1862 he ordered the Government of India to cut its expenditures, especially on education and public works, because of an estimated budget deficit of £284,000.[18] But Lancashire was getting impatient. With the American war then in its second year and prospects for the future gloomy it drew up another memorandum in July in which it reiterated its argument that the Government had a duty to construct public works, such as roads and canals.[19] In response, the Secretary of State resorted to a novel expedient which he thought would soothe the feelings of the cotton interests and at the same time balance the Indian budget. He authorized the Government of India to apply up to £3 million from its cash balances (a sum which resulted from over-borrowing in 1861) to public works such as roads for the transport of cotton.[20]

But to Wood's dismay, the Government of India had already decided to dispose of its cash balances by constructing new barracks for the additional British troops to be stationed in India as part of the new military policy adopted after the Rebellion.[21] And in the interests of a balanced budget – on which Wood had been insisting – it had proposed to cut its expenditure on public works for 1863–64 by more than 13 per cent from the previous year.[22] Wood was aghast at these developments. Lancashire was now persuaded that he was not interested in developing India's resources and had started talk, late in 1862, of impeaching him. As the new parliamentary session got under way in early 1863 – at which he expected trouble – he decided not to let the Government of India dig his political grave. Agitated and determined to protect himself from attack by the cotton interests, he wrote to his old friend, Sir Charles Trevelyan, the Finance Member of the Governor-General's Council:

> You know the state of feeling in this country about all means of facilitating the production and conveyance of cotton. I authorized the expenditure of £3,000,000 for this purpose. We were told that we could not spend it this year for want of superintendence and labour, and were asked to invest it. That is another question, but imagine the insurrection of cotton people that will assuredly take place if I send the money for irrigation, etc. into the gulf of barracks.[23]

Wood again stressed the importance of facilitating the transport of

[18]Secretary of State to Government of India, Despatch no. 83 (Financial), 9 June 1862.
[19]*Proceedings of the Manchester Chamber of Commerce*, 16 July 1862.
[20]Secretary of State to Government of India, Despatch no. 145 (Financial), 30 Aug. 1862. For the reasons for this over-borrowing, see India, *Legislative Council Proceedings*, n.s., II (1863), p. 80, 30 Apr. 1863.
[21]Government of India to Secretary of State, Letter no. 4 (P.W.), 7 Jan. 1863.
[22]Government of India to Secretary of State, Letter no. 5 (P.W.), 7 Jan. 1863.
[23]Wood to Trevelyan, 17 Feb. 1863. Halifax Collection, I. O., Letter Books, XII, p. 82.

cotton by improving communications in India and complained that the Government of India displayed good intentions but little else. The prospects in Lancashire, he reported, were bleak and he would not leave himself open to the charge of trifling with such an important matter.

Wood immediately proceeded to demonstrate to the Government of India his new resolve. Early in March 1863 he informed Trevelyan that any departure from his instructions to spend £3 million from the cash balances on roads and other works in the cotton districts "would be downright disobedience of orders."[24] Within a week he asked Trevelyan to explain why the Government of India was reducing its appropriations for public works in Bombay presidency, one of the major cotton-producing regions of India. "Imagine the outbreak in the House of Commons if it should appear that you have delayed instead of accelerating the construction of these roads."[25] These blunt warnings to Trevelyan reflected Wood's sensitivity to the interests of the politically powerful Lancashire entrepreneurs who were clamouring for an Indian development program. He warned against any reduction of expenditure in Bombay:

> I cannot write too strongly on this point. For heaven's sake do not commit so suicidal an act. I hope that this will be in time to prevent any mischief in your budget statement. I fairly warn you that I shall have no alternative but to express my strong disapprobation of any stint in works of this kind and to throw you over. Stint I mean in money. Exact good work and that is all. The sensible cotton people say they acquit us of any serious neglect, they don't care about the 5 per cent duties, but that we must make roads. They are right but these roads we must make.[26]

Wood was equally blunt with the Governor-General, Lord Elgin: it was "like mockery to spend on barracks money which had been authorized for cotton roads."[27]

The Government of India tried to accommodate itself to the Secretary of State's wishes. Trevelyan promised to make the necessary funds available. In his budget speech to the Legislative Council of India on 30 April 1863, he allocated £2,380,000 for works of public improvement, and an additional sum of £238,000 for cotton roads and other works which could not be built out of the main appropriation.[28] And in reply to Wood's

24Ibid., 5 Mar. 1863, pp. 109–10.
25Ibid., 9 Mar. 1863, p. 118. The Governor of Bombay had complained that his province's grant from imperial revenues for public works had been cut by £100,000 compared with 1862–63.
26Ibid., p. 120.
27Wood to Elgin, 16 Mar. 1863. Halifax Collection, I. O., Letter Books, XII, p. 130.
28India, *Legislative Council Proceedings*, n.s., II (1863), p. 70, 30 Apr. 1863. Trevelyan managed to avoid using the cash balances for public works. Instead, he drew on current revenues and used the extra £3 million in cash balances to reduce the public debt. See ibid., n.s., III (1864), p. 134, 7 Apr. 1864.

accusation that the Government of India's policy had borne few results, Trevelyan prepared a memorandum documenting an impressive program for constructing cotton roads in the two-year period since 1 May 1861. In all, £431,000 had been spent in constructing 4,820 miles of road, 3,220 of which were open for fair weather traffic.[29] More than half of the expenditures was on road construction in Bombay presidency and the Central Provinces – the most important cotton-growing regions of India. In the North-Western Provinces and Punjab, where there were substantial cotton-producing tracts, the problem of road communications was less acute, because good river communications existed.

This unprecedented building of cotton roads was clearly the result of pressure from Lancashire for a communications development program in India. How effective was it? The India Office was skeptical. It believed that the export of cotton had been accelerated by the policies of the Government of India, but privately it expressed the opinion that the cotton districts were still poorly tapped by roads.[30]

This skepticism took insufficient account of the practical problems facing the Government in trying to develop India's road communications. These problems are illustrated by the experiences encountered in a typical road-building project that was designed to link the rich cotton-growing district of Dharwar, in the southern part of Bombay presidency, with the sea at Karwar (then called Sedasheghur), nearly one-hundred miles away. Lancashire was particularly interested in this project because Dharwar was the one part of India where an American variety of cotton had been acclimatized as a result of experiments conducted by the East India Company in the 1840s (see chapter 5). To take advantage of this, a group of Lancashire merchants formed the Manchester Cotton Company in 1860 to purchase cotton in Dharwar and ship it from Karwar directly to Liverpool. The India Office agreed that the Indian authorities would build the necessary road as well as a wharf and other works at the Karwar terminal and the Secretary of State threw his weight behind the project by instructing the Government of India to build the road quickly, regardless of difficulties: "Its completion is . . . an object of so much importance to the cotton trade of this country, that I trust every exertion will be made to effect it at the earliest possible moment."[31]

Unlike many of the other roads listed in Trevelyan's memorandum,

[29]"Public Works for the Purpose of Facilitating the Transit of Cotton to Ports of Shipment: A Memorandum by the Public Works Department, Fort William, 5 June 1863," encl. in Government of India to Secretary of State, Letter no. 48 (P.W.), 16 June 1863.
[30]"Minute in the Public Works Department, India Office, on the Memorandum by the Public Works Department of the Government of India . . . " encl. in Secretary of State to Government of India, Despatch no. 34 (P.W.), 24 Aug. 1863.
[31]Secretary of State to Government of India, Despatch no. 36 (P.W.), 8 Aug. 1861.

which served as feeders for the railways then being constructed, the Dharwar-Karwar road was a major project. Construction, which began in 1861, soon encountered numerous difficulties: labour was hard to procure, the terrain was hazardous, and diseases were endemic. In Dharwar district, where the inhabitants were becoming prosperous from the cultivation of cotton, few sought employment on the road works. In the neighbouring district of North Kanara, through which most of the road was built, population was sparse. The project engineer was therefore dependent for the work of cutting and blasting rocks in the mountains upon labour drawn from wandering tribes, convicts from Dharwar jail, and a company of native sappers and miners. The use of such labour meant that a temporary jail had to be built and the native infantry and police, who acted as escorts for the prisoners, accommodated. Moreover, a good road through the black plains of the Dharwar district had to be built considerably above the level of the land; since gravel was scarce and expensive the embankment had to be constructed of earth, allowed to consolidate during the monsoon rains, covered with gravel, and allowed to consolidate once more. This procedure was time consuming.[32] To add to the difficulties of construction, after the road left Dharwar it entered an almost impenetrable and uninhabited bamboo jungle where wheeled traffic had not been seen before. Supplies could not be purchased locally and workers had to be brought in and then housed, clothed, and fed. All of these conditions added to the costs. Finally, because the area was extremely unhealthy, many coolies deserted. In late December 1862, for example, cholera broke out among 1,850 labourers working on the Kyga Pass through the Western Ghats. Some nine hundred men were stricken and within two days sixteen hundred of the labour force had abandoned their jobs and returned home to Goa and elsewhere. With good cause, one of the engineers compared construction work under these difficult circumstances to a military campaign: "the enemy all along had been the jungle, unseen but felt."[33]

Because the project had been so rushed and was so important, both to the Secretary of State and Lancashire, construction proceeded without plans or cost estimates. In October 1862, the Governor of Bombay remarked that he doubted that the engineers had even chosen the best route. He nevertheless ordered the work to proceed:

> The money value to India is very great, but its value to England cannot be told in money, and every additional thousand bales which we can get down to the sea coast before the season closes in June 1863 may not only save a

[32]Report by the District Engineer, Dharwar, encl. in Government of Bombay to Secretary of State, Letter no. 35 (P.W.), 27 Nov. 1861.

[33]Report by the District Engineer, Dharwar, encl. in Government of Bombay to Secretary of State, Letter no. 70 (P.W.), 9 Nov. 1866.

score of weavers from starvation or crime but may play an important part in ensuring peace and prosperity to the manufacturing districts of more than one country in Europe.[34]

The engineers were accordingly authorized to use whatever money they could "economically, fairly, and honestly." By the end of 1864 over £50,000 had been spent; but even though the whole force of the Bombay public works department was brought to bear on the works, progress was slow. By 1865 the road had been opened during the dry season for light-wheeled traffic only. The end of the American Civil War undermined the principal reason for building the road, but it could not now be abandoned half-finished; it was not yet metalled, and, as a result, after each monsoon it required extensive repairs. In order to cut costs the width of the road to be metalled was reduced from twenty-seven feet to sixteen feet. Even so, total outlays on this project came to just under £100,000.

Equally dismal was the story of the effort to construct a new deep-sea port at the terminus of the road at Karwar. Plans and surveys for this project had been under discussion in India for several years but no action was taken until 1861 because of lack of funds. However, when a deputation of directors of the newly formed Manchester Cotton Company visited Wood in March 1861 to explain their plans, he assured them that the Madras government intended to construct a pier at Karwar during the current year and that it would be ready at the same time as the road linking the port with Dharwar.[35] Wood expected the Madras government to proceed expeditiously with the proposed works; but there was an administrative obstacle whose removal would, he believed, ensure their more rapid completion. Karwar was situated in the North Kanara district of Madras presidency but its cotton-growing hinterland formed part of Bombay. This meant that Madras was responsible for developing plans and allocating funds for the port works and the section of the connecting road to Dharwar up to the district boundary, while the Bombay government had a similar responsibility for the section of road in its territory. This led to difficulties over choice of route and priority in allocating funds between the two presidencies. Wood came to the conclusion, which was shared by the Bombay government, that the cotton-growing districts which formed the hinterland to the port, the roads from the districts to the proposed port, and the port itself should be under the same administration. In January 1861 he authorized the Governor-General of India to transfer the

---

[34]Minute by the Governor of Bombay, 22 Oct. 1862, encl. in Government of Bombay to Secretary of State, Letter no. 15 (P.W.), 24 Nov. 1862.

[35]The deputation met Wood on 15 March. The written confirmation was sent in Under-Secretary of State to Manchester Cotton Company, 12 Apr. 1861. India Office, Public Works Department, Home Correspondence, B, I, 39.

district of North Kanara to Bombay unless there were insuperable obstacles to the change.[36]

- Not only did the Madras government oppose the transfer; but it was also violently opposed to the proposal to construct port facilities at Karwar. In May 1861 the Governor, Sir William Denison, who was an engineer by training, wrote a stinging Minute in which he condemned the whole scheme as "most wildly conceived." But when he received a despatch from London ordering rapid completion he reluctantly gave the necessary orders. He was convinced that the difficulties could be overcome only at excessive cost, and that even then there would be little or no traffic to justify the expenditure. Because of the importance attached to the scheme by the Secretary of State, who was anxious to do everything possible to assist the Manchester Cotton Company, he allowed the works to proceed without a properly prepared plan and without estimates of cost.[37] In October 1861, after personally visiting the works, he altered the plans and thereby caused further delay. He also wrote to the Governor of Bombay, to whose jurisdiction the district was about to be transferred, warning him not to construct any large works since a few ships would suffice to carry off all the exportable produce and fewer still to bring in the articles required by the people in the back country.[38]

While these difficulties were occurring in India, the Manchester Cotton Company was having its own difficulties in England. The Company had been formed in January 1861 with a nominal capital of £1 million, but up to 31 July 1862 only £41,900 had been raised. This was a telling illustration of Lancashire's skepticism of India as a permanent source of cotton supply, referred to in an earlier chapter. Not only had the Company been unsuccessful in raising sufficient capital; but it had itself failed to import any cotton from India and had spent most of the money it had been able to raise in sending a shipload of cleaning and pressing machinery to Karwar, where it arrived just as the monsoon was about to break. There was nowhere to put the machinery except on the shore and there it rusted for nearly a year. The Company blamed the government for not having the promised pier ready, and Wood had to admit that this was so and that the roads were inadequate.[39] But he disclaimed any responsibility on the part of the government and rejected a claim for £20,000 compensation which the

[36]Wood to Canning, 23 Jan. 1861. Halifax Collection, I. O., Letter Books, VI, p. 76.

[37]Sir W. Denison, *Varieties of Viceregal Life,* 2 vols. (London: Longmans, Green, 1870), II, p. 85. Denison maintained his opposition to the transfer of North Kanara to Bombay which he delayed for a year until ordered to transfer the district by Wood in February 1862.

[38]Ibid., p. 125.

[39]Wood to Hugh Mason, Chairman, Manchester Cotton Company, 5 Nov. 1862. Halifax Collection, I. O., Letter Books, XI, pp. 246–47.

directors of the Company submitted in January 1863.[40] Meanwhile, the Company had still failed to import any cotton from India; because of this, the cotton-pressing machinery, when it was finally set up in Karwar and Dharwar, lay idle. In 1864 the directors were unsuccessful in an effort to raise more capital for the Company and in August it went into voluntary liquidation.[41]

While the Manchester Cotton Company was foundering, work at Karwar continued; by 30 April 1865 £115,000 had been spent in India and £10,362 in England on the port. In addition to the £100,000 spent on the connecting road to Dharwar, nearly a quarter of a million pounds had been spent on works which officials on the spot had warned would not bring any return and whose principal justification was the desire of the India Office to help a Lancashire joint-stock company develop a new source of raw material for an industry determined to look elsewhere than India for the bulk of its supplies.

The port and road works in North Kanara were designed to facilitate the export of cotton from the Dharwar district in the southern part of the Bombay presidency, to the west coast at Karwar. Another extensive project undertaken in the mid-nineteenth century under pressure from the Lancashire cotton interests was the Godavari river navigation scheme. This was designed to provide cheap water transport to the east coast for the cotton of Nagpur and Berar in Central India, territories which had been annexed by the British with an eye to their cotton-exporting potential.[42]

The Godavari rises in western India and flows for nine hundred miles across the Deccan in a south-easterly direction. With its tributaries, it forms a river network 2,610 miles long. However, only 473 miles were navigable and even this portion was not naturally navigable for more than five months of the year, when the system was fed by the monsoon rains. In addition, navigation was impeded by three major falls of rock in the river bed. Despite these handicaps of climate and geology, high hopes were held that the Godavari could be turned into a great navigable waterway. Sir Charles Wood predicted in the House of Commons in August 1854 that if the river proved navigable, it might open up one of the greatest cotton districts in India and enable cotton to be secured at a cheaper rate than any railway.[43]

---

[40]Under-Secretary of State to Manchester Cotton Company, 19 Feb. 1863. I. O., P.W. Dept., Home Corresp., B, II, p. 22; Manchester Cotton Company to Under-Secretary of State, 23 Mar. 1863. Ibid., A, IX, 17/23. The Government of Bombay paid the Company £450 for a pier it had constructed at Karwar. The Government thought this was far more than the pier was worth but paid it in order to end lengthy discussion of the matter. See Government of Bombay to Secretary of State, Letter no. 53 (P.W.), 4 Nov. 1863.
[41]Public Record Office (London), BT 31/549, No. 2224.
[42]See chapter 1, note 12.
[43]*Parl. Deb.,* 3rd ser., CXXXV, col. 1454, 8 Aug. 1854.

With this encouragement from London, surveys were carried out in 1855, and as a result of them, an ambitious plan was presented for the construction of canals with locks, dams for the storage of water, and various ancillary works which would open the Godavari to steam navigation for a distance of 473 miles from the sea for seven months of the year, with the possibility of year-round navigation if storage reservoirs were constructed at the heads of the various rivers of the system.[44] The Madras government, in whose jurisdiction the major part of the Godavari system lay, was initially enthusiastic over the economic and social benefits which would result from this scheme, particularly the export of cotton to England. It sent the engineer who had submitted the plans, F. T. Haig, to Europe and America to inspect river navigation works and to gain experience in their operation; and it proposed to London acceptance of Haig's scheme to open navigation for seven months of the year. The cost was estimated at £292,500.[45] The Court of Directors approved but the outbreak of the Rebellion in 1857 delayed formal sanction until June 1858. By then, India's financial difficulties caused the Government of India to withhold its permission. In Lancashire, however, the Cotton Supply Association was anxious·to see the scheme proceed and was exerting pressure on Sir Charles Wood to use his authority to get things going.[46] In India, the Governor of Madras, Sir Charles Trevelyan, a close friend of Wood, was an ardent supporter of the scheme. He believed in the superiority of water over rail transport and predicted that opening up the Godavari would create a new trade of limitless extent, with a small outlay compared with the results to be achieved.[47]

[44]F. T. Haig, *Report on the Navigability of the River Godavari and Some of its Affluents* (Madras, 1856), p. 31.

[45]Madras, Public Works Consultations, 19 May 1857, no. 961. Haig's own enthusiasm for the Godavari scheme was motivated by Christianity not cotton. He had developed strong religious feelings as a youth. Soon after he began work on the irrigation works being constructed in the Godavari delta by Arthur Cotton he "experienced that great change of attitude towards God which Our Blessed Lord described as being 'born again'." C. A. Haig, *Memories of the Life of General F. T. Haig by His Wife* (London: Marshall Bros., 1902), p. 9. In 1857, during the early stages of the navigation project, Haig was preaching to his workers and to the villagers. In 1861 he persuaded the Church Missionary Society to establish a mission on the Godavari. His wife states that despite the eventual abandonment of the navigation scheme, "in God's providence the engineering work had been used to pave the way for His own blessed work of gathering the heathen into the Kingdom of Christ." Ibid., p. 29. Haig returned to the Godavari in 1881, after his retirement from government service, and spent a year in charge of a mission station. He later carried on missionary work in Arabia.

[46]*Cotton Supply Reporter*, 1 June 1859.

[47]Minute by Sir Charles Trevelyan, 15 Oct. 1859, encl. in Government of Madras to Secretary of State, Letter no. 51 (P.W.), 25 Sept. 1859. Trevelyan, with more foresight than he knew, drew a parallel between the Godavari navigation scheme and the navigation works on the river Shannon in Ireland where, although "the absence of trade and the introduction of railroads have prevented the realization of the results expected from

In these circumstances, Wood gave his sanction in January 1860 and the Government of India allocated the first instalment of the necessary funds later in the year. It did so reluctantly because its experts did not share the enthusiasm of Trevelyan, Wood, or the Cotton Supply Association for the possibilities of successful navigation on the Godavari. Moreover, it was still concerned about the state of the Indian finances. In fact, the fear that the Government of India's financial difficulties might prevent it from vigorously prosecuting the works led a group of Lancashire manufacturers led by J. B. Smith, the member of Parliament for Stockport, to propose turning the scheme over to private enterprise. Smith was a prominent member of the Manchester School, whose energetic participation in the campaign to repeal the Corn Laws in the 1840s had earned him the title of "Corn Law Smith." His determination in pressing for construction of the Godavari waterway in the 1860s was to win him the soubriquet of "Godavari Smith." Smith's group now offered to put up £300,000 to finance the project provided they received a guaranteed interest of five per cent and various other privileges.[48] Wood was prepared to enter into negotiations but when, early in 1861, he interviewed half a dozen of the leading manufacturers who were behind the scheme he found that they were not, after all, prepared to do anything. John Bright tried to put pressure on them without success. Just as they failed to provide sufficient capital for the Manchester Cotton Company, so the cotton manufacturers were unwilling to invest money in the Godavari development scheme. Wood reluctantly concluded that private enterprise could not be counted on to develop the Godavari.[49]

By now the Madras government had lost its enthusiasm. In February 1861, Sir William Denison became Governor. He examined the plans for the project; concluded that the estimates were too low, the engineering designs incomplete, and the traffic projections over-optimistic; and recommended instead the execution of temporary works to link the navigable sections of the river by means of inexpensive roads. This, he considered, would be in keeping with the Government of India's own policy that proposals from the provincial governments to stimulate the production and export of cotton must relate to the 1861–62 season. This

this system of works, it is one of the most complete of its kind in existence." The same factors—absence of trade and the introduction of railways—were to contribute to the failure of the Godavari scheme. Soon after Trevelyan made this prediction, the *Report on Railways in India to the End of 1859* correctly forecast that the penetration of Berar by the railway would tap the cotton resources of that region. See *Parl. Papers*, LII (1860), No. 2669, p. 47. In spite of this forecast by one of his own officials, Wood pressed on with the project.

[48]Secretary of State to Government of India, Despatch no. 50 (P.W.), 6 July 1860.
[49]Wood to Canning, 26 Feb. 1861, and to W. A. Morehead, Acting-Governor of Madras, 26 Feb. 1861. Halifax Collection, I. O., Letter Books, VI, pp. 194 and 224.

specifically excluded long-term projects such as railway or canal construction.[50]

Denison's caution, born of his engineering experience, was unwelcome to both the Indian and the British Governments. The Government of India was being exhorted to get on with the job by Wood, who in turn was under pressure from the Lancashire lobby in Parliament, led by J. B. Smith.[51] On 25 July 1861, Wood announced in Parliament that, in order to expedite the supply of cotton from Berar, no time would be lost in developing the Godavari. He stated that in the precarious state of the cotton supply, the Government would be failing in its duty to Great Britain and India if it did not take energetic measures to provide the means of communications between the cotton-growing districts and the coast.[52] Wood's public declaration of intention to improve India's communications was reinforced in both his official and private correspondence. In a despatch to the Government of India in August, he stressed "the indirect effect which they cannot fail to have in contributing most materially to the supply of the English cotton market,"[53] and he privately told Canning, the Governor-General, that although he thought Haig's rough estimates of the cost of the navigation scheme were probably too low, he was quite ready to spend up to one million pounds if necessary.[54] Wood was determined that the cotton manufacturers would not be able to accuse him of indifference, even though he privately doubted that they would avail themselves of anything that was done.[55]

Despite Wood's insistence that the Godavari works should proceed, officials in India were increasingly reluctant. Denison visited the Godavari in July 1861, and in November he repeated his doubts about the practicability of the scheme in a despatch to London.[56] Wood maintained his belief in the scheme, but by now the Government of India was having second thoughts.[57] It sent one of its officials, Richard Temple, to visit Nagpur and Central India in the summer of 1861. He reported that all government officials he had talked to agreed with the view of the Bombay merchants, both European and Indian, that the Godavari could never compete for the cotton of Berar with the railway then under construction from Bombay to

[50]Denison, op. cit., II, p. 84; Government of Madras to Government of India, no. 1136, 21 June 1861, and to Secretary of State, Letter no. 57 (P.W.), 21 June 1861.
[51]The Godavari scheme was raised in Parliament on 5 July 1861. On 24 July a deputation of twenty-two members of Parliament, led by Smith, visited Wood and discussed the matter with him. *Cotton Supply Reporter,* 1 Aug. 1861.
[52]*Parl. Deb.,* 3rd ser., CLXIV, col. 1519, 25 July 1861.
[53]Secretary of State to Government of India, Despatch no. 39 (P.W.), 2 Aug. 1861.
[54]Wood to Canning, 3 Aug. 1861. Halifax Collection, I. O., Letter Books, VIII, p. 146.
[55]Wood to Denison, 18 Aug. 1861. Halifax Collection, I. O., Letter Books, VIII, p. 206.
[56]Denison to Wood, 13 Sept. 1861. Halifax Collection, I. O., Corresp. India; Government of Madras to Secretary of State, Letter no. 76 (P.W.), 4 Nov. 1861.
[57]Secretary of State to Government of Madras, Despatch no. 2 (P.W.), 8 Feb. 1862.

Nagpur. "On the whole, as far as present appearances go, it seems doubtful whether the existing cotton fields will be immediately benefited by the opening of the Godavari."[58]

In this atmosphere of doubt, work proceeded on the Godavari under Haig's direction. In England, the Godavari lobby was complaining about lack of progress; and in January 1862 a deputation from the Cotton Supply Association, led by J. B. Smith, visited Lord Elgin, who was about to leave the country to take office as Governor-General of India, to impress upon him the importance they attached to the scheme. Smith claimed that the Godavari would become for the cotton of Berar what the Mississippi was for the cotton of the American South. He also criticized the Government of India for slowing down the works by its policy, which was fully in keeping with the principles of *laissez-faire*, of financing development out of current revenue instead of borrowing for the purpose.[59]

In fact, more important than finances in holding up progress were the same kind of difficulties experienced in building the Dharwar-Karwar road: scarcity of labour, difficulty of terrain, and cholera.[60] There was another similarity between the two projects: division of administrative responsibility, this time between the Madras government, which as a presidency government had the right of direct access to the Secretary of State, and the Government of India, which had to sanction all expenditures on public works made by subordinate governments. To resolve the latter problem, responsibility for the navigation works was transferred on 1 May 1863 to the recently-created Central Provinces, which were directly under the Government of India. In anticipation of the transfer, the Chief Commissioner of the Central Provinces, Richard Temple, travelled along the entire navigable valley of the Godavari in August and September 1862. His report to the Government of India in January 1863 cast new doubts on the navigation scheme. Not only did Temple stress the climatic difficulties which detracted from the value of the scheme, but he also drew attention to an important factor affecting the prospects of cotton exports along the Godavari. Cotton was ready for export from Nagpur in March, whereas, at best, the Godavari navigation would not be open until the monsoon broke some time in June. This would give the railway a decisive advantage over the waterway as a means of exporting cotton. Temple concluded that for this reason cotton should not be counted on as an important factor in future Godavari traffic.[61]

[58]Temple to Private Secretary to Governor-General, 18 Sept. 1861. Canning Papers, 108/9339.

[59]*Cotton Supply Reporter*, 1 Feb. 1862.

[60]Government of Madras to Secretary of State, Letters no. 23 and no. 60 (P.W.), 11 Apr. and 14 July 1862.

[61]Memorandum by R. Temple, 20 Aug. 1862; Report on the Godavari by R. Temple,

Temple also reported on the financing of the project and progress so far made. He recommended the adoption of a much more limited scheme, involving opening navigation for only 300 miles instead of 473 miles as originally planned; even this would cost between £390,000 and £440,000, compared with Haig's original estimate of only £290,000 for the more ambitious project. The Government of India agreed, having been warned not to believe in "any romance of the cotton trade down the Godavari" by its senior public works official, Colonel Richard Strachey.[62] This cutback alarmed Sir Charles Wood, who asked for a progress report. The news he received was not encouraging: plans and estimates, when Haig finally submitted them to the Government of India in 1864, were rejected as useless.[63] Sir John Lawrence, the Governor-General, thereupon ordered a reappraisal of the entire scheme. He reminded Wood that it had been undertaken solely in response to agitation in Parliament and at Wood's own orders but that few in India believed that it was worth the cost it would entail.[64]

While the review was being carried out, cholera killed 800 of the work force and many others fled. Operations had to be suspended and when the scattered work force was again collected, only 2,500 of the original 6,000 reappeared.[65] When the review was completed in September 1865, it showed that while expenditures of £286,000 had already been incurred, at least £520,000 more would have to be spent even to complete Temple's limited scheme adopted two years previously. The Governor-General's Council was opposed to such a heavy outlay.[66] But Lawrence – although he thought it was a "great misfortune" that the scheme had ever been undertaken – feared to draw back after so much money had been spent and in view of the known wishes of the Secretary of State. So the Government of India decided to throw good money after bad and ordered continuation of the limited project.[67] Wood, however, insisted on construction

---

23 Jan. 1863, encl. in Government of India to Secretary of State, Letter no. 79 (P.W.), 9 Dec. 1863.

[62]Col. R. Strachey, Secretary to the Government of India in the Public Works Dept., to Temple, 28 Oct. 1862. Richard Temple Collection (India Office Library, MSS. Eur. F. 86), no. 54 (Special Letters, Central Provinces, 1862–67); Government of India to Secretary of State, Letter no. 79 (P.W.), 9 Dec. 1863.

[63]Government of India to Secretary of State, Letter no. 59 (P.W.), 4 Aug. 1864.

[64]Lawrence to Wood, 16 June 1864. Halifax Collection, I. O., Corresp., India.

[65]*Report on the Administration of the Central Provinces, 1864–65* (Nagpur, 1865), para. 139.

[66]Note by Col. H. Durand, 26 Aug. 1865, encl. in Government of India to Secretary of State, Letter no. 116 (P.W.), 13 Sept. 1865.

[67]Ibid. Several years later, Richard Strachey, who drafted this despatch, said that "it was not considered either decent or necessary to refer in it in an offensive way to the action of the Secretary of State in connection with these works, which had, as I think, more or less been opposed to the wishes of the Government of India. The Government of India did not wish to write anything that might be disagreeable to the Secretary

of the entire scheme because he feared that otherwise the Godavari waterway would never be able to compete with the railway for the cotton traffic of central India.[68] However, Wood resigned as Secretary of State in February 1866 soon after issuing these orders and the Government of India decided to take no action on them pending yet another review, this time by its engineers. They recommended scaling down the project to make the Godavari fit for navigation only by native boats instead of steamers.[69]

A majority of the Governor-General's Council now wanted to abandon the navigation scheme altogether.[70] The railway from Bombay to Nagpur had been completed in February 1867 and was now transporting the cotton crop of Nagpur to the coast. In the North-Western Provinces, merchants were paying high freight rates to export cotton from Allahabad by rail rather than sending it down the Ganges in steamers or native boats.[71] Lawrence was in a quandary and did not know what to do, but in London opinion was now hardening against the project. The American war was over, Lancashire was turning once more to the United States for its cotton supplies, and interest in Indian cotton was diminishing. In London, the new Conservative Secretary of State, Sir Stafford Northcote, was ready to accept a recommendation from the Government of India for abandonment of the works and to face the clamour that would arise.[72] But Lawrence, who had been on the Secretary of State's Council in 1861 when Wood had given in to pressure from Lancashire and had ordered construction of the navigation works, shrank from so bold a decision although he admitted that no member of his Council would say a word in opposition to abandonment.[73]

---

of State, there was no object in doing so, or in laying stress upon these facts." *Report from the Select Committee on East India Finances*, in *Parl. Papers*, VIII (1872), No. 327, Minutes of Evidence, Q. 7089.

[68]Secretary of State to Government of India, Despatch no. 11 (P.W.), 8 Feb. 1866.

[69]Report by Colonels Anderson and Fife, 27 June 1866, encl. in Government of India to Secretary of State, Letter no. 36 (P.W.), 8 Mar. 1867. One reason for their rejection of steam navigation was the fact that Haig had designed locks of 30 feet width for use by stern-wheelers of the type common on American rivers. They considered that such steamers would not be suitable in the currents and whirlpools encountered on the Godavari and they thought that sidewheelers would not be sufficiently powerful against the river's current.

[70]W. Grey, H. S. M. Maine, General Sir H. W. Norman, and Sir H. Durand. National Archives of India, India, Public Works (Civil Works, Communications) Proceedings, April 1867, nos. 1–16.

[71]Minute by Colonel Sir H. Durand, 23 Feb. 1867, encl. in Government of India to Secretary of State, Letter no. 36 (P.W.), 8 Mar. 1867.

[72]Northcote to Lawrence, 9 June 1867. John Lawrence Collection, Letters from the Secretary of State, XXVIII, no. 29.

[73]Lawrence to Northcote, 18 July 1867. John Lawrence Collection, Letters to the Secretary of State, XXXII, no. 43. Lawrence had, of course, inaugurated a vast scheme of irrigation works as Chief Commissioner of the Punjab before the Rebellion. This may have inclined him towards continuation of the Godavari scheme.

So in September 1867, it was decided to carry on with the scheme in its entirety: the Godavari would be opened to steam navigation along its entire navigable length of 473 miles. In Northcote's view, there could be no half measures; it must be all or nothing.[74] This policy caused consternation in the Government of India, which strongly protested the decision; but in February 1868 Northcote overruled its objections, and when the Indian authorities again demurred, the Home Government insisted on its orders being carried out.[75] However, in July the first locks on the Godavari were completed and navigation opened for a distance of more than 200 miles from the sea. The traffic results of the first year of operations then bore out all the forecasts of the pessimists. Moreover, navigation through the canal and beyond became impossible after October 15 because the water level in the river fell so low. The only traffic during the three months of operations consisted of government boats carrying stores for the navigation works further up the river. There was no traffic in cotton.[76] Results were equally bad in 1869-70.

These were disappointing results, and further financial difficulties were to be expected.[77] Consequently, the Government of India recommended abandonment of the Godavari navigation scheme to the Secretary of State in June 1871.[78] At first, the recommendation was rejected. The Liberals were back in power in England and the Secretary of State, the Duke of Argyll, reverted to the limited scheme adopted by the Government of India in 1863 on the advice of Richard Temple.[79] But the Government of India then had an unexpected piece of luck. Surveys and estimates were under way for a railway to tap the coal and iron resources which had been discovered along the Wardha river, one of the tributaries of the Godavari, in 1868. The Wardha valley was also an important cotton-growing area, which added to the attractiveness of the proposed railway. Then in September 1871, the Government of India received word that coal had also been discovered on the lower Godavari, below the locks which had been opened in July 1868. Lord Mayo, the Governor-General, at once saw the significance of this discovery. "If true," he noted, "this ought to settle

[74]Secretary of State to Government of India, Despatch no. 86 (P.W.), 14 Sept. 1867.

[75]Government of India to Secretary of State, Letter no. 68 (P.W.), 22 Apr. 1868; Secretary of State to Government of India, Despatch no. 63 (P.W.), 25 June 1868.

[76]NAI, India, P.W. (Communications) Procs., December 1869, no. 38.

[77]There were budget deficits in four consecutive years from 1866–67 to 1869–70 and the accumulated deficit over this period amounted to £10,753,236. *Statistical Abstract Relating to British India from 1863 to 1872*, in *Parl. Papers*, LXIX (1873), C. 870, p. 2.

[78]Government of India to Secretary of State, Letter no. 63 (P.W.), 1 June 1871. Sir Richard Temple, alone of the Governor-General's Council, dissented from this recommendation.

[79]Secretary of State to Government of India, Despatch no. 59 (P.W.), 22 Aug. 1871.

the Upper Godavari folly."[80] When Mayo received confirmation of the discovery he telegraphed to the Secretary of State, asking if the news would alter his decision to go on with the useless navigation works. Argyll gave way, for the case for a railway which would tap both the coal and cotton resources of the Wardha valley was now beyond dispute.[81] He authorized the abandonment of the works and the Government of India issued the necessary instructions on 22 November 1872.

So ended the effort, sustained over nearly two decades, to turn the Godavari into a navigable waterway. The object of the scheme was to tap a new source of raw cotton for British industry, and it was undertaken in response to pressure from the Manchester School in the 1850s for a more vigorous public works policy to develop India's resources. In the early 1860s it received a powerful stimulus from the outbreak of civil war in America. Subsequently it was pursued partly in order to demonstrate to Lancashire the British Government's continuing concern to secure alternative sources of raw cotton; and partly because the expenditures were so great, measured by the standards of the time, that the only justification for them in a period of financial difficulty for the Government of India was the successful completion of the project. In all, £750,000 was spent in this further demonstration of the power of the so-called free traders to influence government policy in the interests of the Lancashire cotton industry. India benefited not at all, since the project was a complete failure.

In the field of railway construction in India in the mid-nineteenth century, the influence of Lancashire was equally clear. The Lancashire cotton interests played an important role in the adoption of the guarantee system, whereby companies given contracts to build railways in India were guaranteed interest of five per cent on capital outlay. The first Indian railway company to ask for such a guarantee was the Great Indian Peninsula, which proposed to connect Bombay with Nagpur. This was a line in which Lancashire had a particular interest since it would tap rich cotton-growing districts. Commercial groups in Manchester and elsewhere lent powerful support to the efforts of the promoters of this company to secure a guarantee.[82] Ironically, it was one of the earliest advocates of free trade in Great Britain and an outstanding member of the Manchester

[80]NAI, India, P.W. (Bridges and Roads, Communications) Procs., December 1871, nos. 1–7, "Keep-With" Note by Lord Mayo, 29 Sept. 1871.

[81]The Chief Commissioner of the Central Provinces argued that construction of a railway would not only secure the more rapid export of raw cotton but would also lower the cost of imported Lancashire piece goods. This in turn would divert labour from spinning and weaving to agriculture and so lead to an extension of the area under cultivation. See *Report on the Administration of the Central Provinces, 1868–69* (Nagpur, 1869), para. 202; and ibid., 1869–70 (Nagpur, 1870), paras. 117 and 162.

[82]See Thorner, op. cit., ch. 6 for the struggle for the guarantee and the role of the Lancashire cotton interests.

School, James Wilson, who produced the formula in 1849 which formed the basis of the guaranteed contracts between the East India Company and the railway companies.[83]

The founder of the G.I.P. railway, John Chapman, had actually been sent to India in 1845 by the Lancashire cotton interests in order to promote the company's objects and to seek the support of the Bombay government.[84] In 1851, after the battle of the guarantee had been won, Chapman wrote a book of which the very title, *The Cotton and Commerce of India Considered in Relation to the Interests of Great Britain; With Remarks on Railway Communication in the Bombay Presidency*, shows the close connection between cotton and railways in India. In it, he warned of the dangers to British exports of increasing industrialization in Europe and America and stressed the advantages of developing new markets in the empire.[85] The Manchester manufacturers were receptive to such arguments: railway construction would facilitate the export of their products to India as well as opening up new sources of raw materials for their factories. They became active proponents of railway construction and their influence can be seen not only in the case of the G.I.P. but also in the cases of the Bombay, Baroda, and Central India Railway, linking Bombay with Surat and Ahmedabad and so tapping the cotton districts of Gujarat; and the Great Southern Railway, which passed through the cotton districts of Madras.[86]

But Lancashire's willingness to exert pressure to secure guarantees for railways which would open up cotton-growing regions of India was not matched by equal willingness to invest capital in these railways. The five per cent guarantee was not enough to attract speculative risk-taking capitalists such as the Manchester merchants and manufacturers, who were busy overstocking the Indian market with their products in the years 1858–61.[87] The chairman of the East India Railway Company complained at the annual meeting of shareholders in May 1861 how little support his company and the G.I.P. railway had had from Manchester.[88] Those who

[83]Ibid., pp. 159 and 166–67. Wilson, who became secretary to the Board of Control in 1848, was founder and first editor of *The Economist*. He served as Finance Member of the Governor-General's Council in 1859–60 and in that capacity angered his Manchester friends by raising the Indian cotton duties.

[84]This was stated by William Sowerby, who went to India in 1854 as assistant engineer for the E.I.R. and spent the next twenty-five years in India as engineer, surveyor, and contractor. See *Report from the Select Committee on East India (Public Works)*, in *Parl. Papers*, IX (1878–79), No. 312, Minutes of Evidence, Q. 217.

[85]MacPherson, op. cit., p. 183.

[86]Ibid., p. 184.

[87]Eugene A. Brady, "A Reconsideration of the Lancashire 'Cotton Famine'," *Agricultural History*, XXXVII (1963), pp. 158–60. A powerful Lancashire deputation admitted as much to the Prime Minister and Wood in 1862. See above, p. 23.

[88]*The Times*, 1 May 1861.

did provide most of the capital were British middle class investors of the cautious, safety-seeking kind – widows, barristers, clergymen, spinsters, bankers, and retired army officers.[89]

The outflow of British capital for construction of railways in India in the 1860s was considerable, as shown in Table 4.1. It is a further measure

Table 4.1
Capital Expenditure on Indian Railways, 1858–69

Year	Amount (£)	Year	Amount (£)
1858	5,492,108	1864	4,122,240
1859	7,171,464	1865	5,636,866
1860	7,578,715	1866	7,297,763
1861	6,602,212	1867	7,120,875
1862	5,863,000	1868	4,420,325
1863	4,755,653	1869	4,933,721

SOURCE: *Report from the Select Committee on East India (Public Works)*, in *Parliamentary Papers* (1878–79), IX, No. 312, p. v.

of the casuistry of the Manchester School that while the Lancashire cotton interests loudly demanded extensive railway construction under government guarantee in India in the mid-nineteenth century in order to expedite the transport of cotton, they also complained that the resulting outflow of capital raised interest rates in Britain to the detriment of the country's trade (see above, p. 28). They then used this as an argument for abolition of the Indian cotton duties even though this would reduce the revenue of the Government of India. At the same time, when the Government of India's financial difficulties in the aftermath of the Rebellion caused Sir Charles Wood to resist extending further guarantees to private enterprises, such as railway and irrigation companies, there were loud complaints from Lancashire and talk of impeaching the Secretary of State.[90]

The way in which these large expenditures on railways and other public works were financed in this period caused considerable difficulty for the Government of India. The practice was to debit revenue with capital charges, in keeping with the view, strongly held by free traders such as Sir Charles Wood and Sir Charles Trevelyan, that government expenditure on public works was justifiable only if the revenue benefited in the shape of a cash return on investment. In 1865 Wood reminded

[89]MacPherson, op. cit., p. 181.
[90]R. J. Moore, *Sir Charles Wood's Indian Policy, 1853–66*, p. 147, and see above, p. 30.

Trevelyan's successor as Finance Member of the Governor-General's Council, W. N. Massey, of this: "Trevelyan laid down in the most absolute way the principle of providing for the annual expenditure on public works out of Income, and if it could be done, I was too glad to see such a safe principle of finance acted on."[91] But from 1866 on, the Government of India began to incur a series of budgetary deficits. This prompted the Radical member of Parliament, Henry Fawcett, to protest in Parliament at the way in which Indian finances were being sacrificed to British considerations.[92] As a result of Fawcett's criticisms, Select Committees on Indian Finances were appointed in 1871, 1872, 1873, and 1874. Fawcett's work on these committees revealed, among other things, the waste of public funds on the Godavari navigation scheme. But his services extended further:

> His careful study of the often very involved public accounts of India over the previous decade frequently enabled him to reveal other serious instances of wasteful or dubious expenditure, nearly all indicative of Britain's bland disregard of India's terrible poverty whenever its own interests were at stake.[93]

This modern view of the nature of the relationship between Britain and India in the mid-nineteenth century is no more than a restatement of the case as put in 1862 by Samuel Laing, whose candour in revealing Britain's imperial interests in India while he was Finance Member has already been noted. Writing in *The Times* on the subject of Indian finances in May 1870 Laing said:

> If India were an independent country, or even an independent colony like Canada, she would undoubtedly do as Canada has done – that is, when pressed for money increase import duties. Rather than impose an income tax, it is absolutely certain that India, if left to herself, would raise the import duty on British manufactures to the point which would give the largest revenue, say, to 15 or 20 per cent. But how would Lancashire like that?[94]

An earlier chapter has demonstrated Lancashire's strong feelings on the tariff. The present chapter has shown Lancashire's attitude to public works. The two are related. The cotton interests demanded extensive public works in India in the mid-nineteenth century – roads, railways, canals, and

---

91Wood to Massey, 15 May 1865. Halifax Collection, I. O., Letter Books, XX, p. 9.
92*Parl. Deb.,* 3rd ser., CCIII, col. 1605, 5 Aug. 1870. For expenditures on major public works, irrigation, and railways in India from 1857 to 1870, see Silver, op. cit., pp. 126–27.
93S. Maccoby, *English Radicalism, 1853–1886* (London: Allen and Unwin, 1938), p. 371.
94*The Times*, 23 May 1870.

irrigation schemes – and, despite their adherence to the principles of *laissez-faire*, they demanded that the government should carry them out. But they also resisted any attempt by government to increase its income by raising the import duties, because this was contrary to free trade principles. The funds for public works came from current revenues, and many of these works were undertaken in response to political pressure from Lancashire and against the advice of the authorities in India. Until 1868 railways were constructed with capital raised in England at guaranteed rates of interest, a system which by no means necessarily served India's best interests, but which Lancashire was instrumental in securing.[95] Lancashire's desire to secure a new source of raw material was behind much of the public works and railway policy of the Government of India in the mid-nineteenth century. And Lancashire's desire that the cotton obtained from India should be equal in quality to American cotton was behind the Government of India's cotton improvement program in the same period.

[95]Leland H. Jenks, *The Migration of British Capital to 1875* (New York: Alfred Knopf, 1927), pp. 220–22.

5

THE STATE AND COTTON IMPROVEMENT
Agricultural Aspects, 1863–75

"THE DUTY OF THE GOVERNMENT to inaugurate and stimulate improvements in cultivating the soil, and directing industrial pursuits, has long been admitted, and . . . it is submitted that there can be no case more important and none of equal urgency, in which this principle should be carried out, than in the improvement of the quality and increase of the quantity of cotton grown in India."[1] So argued the Cotton Supply Association in August 1869, repeating a demand for government action to improve the quality of Indian cotton, thereby making it more suitable for Lancashire's mills, which went back forty years. The East India Company had first undertaken experimental cultivation of cotton as early as 1829 and had continued experiments for a number of years thereafter. But the results were unsatisfactory and the experiments were abandoned. The commercial slump in England in 1836 stimulated new demands from cotton manufacturers for action by the East India Company to develop India as a source of cotton which could compete with the United States. But Indian cotton could only compete with American cotton if it were improved in quality. Under pressure from Lancashire, the East India Company launched a cotton improvement program in 1840 which was designed to

[1]Cotton Supply Association to Under-Secretary of State, 4 Aug. 1869. India Office, Home Correspondence, Letters Received, X, no. 1234.

encourage Indian cultivators to plant more cotton; to teach them to improve their methods of growing, picking, and cleaning it; and to introduce
new varieties of long-stapled cotton into the country. This program failed,
partly for reasons of soil and climate, but also because little attention was
paid to economic, cultural, and social factors which were basic elements
in the structure of Indian agriculture. The experimental cultivation of
American cotton, under the direction of American planters brought
specially to India for the purpose, had little relevance to the problems
faced by the cultivators in growing and marketing cotton. Their indebted-
ness to the village moneylender, to whom they mortgaged their crop in
return for loans to buy seed, removed a possible incentive for careful
cultivation or clean picking of cotton. The indigenous plants which they
cultivated were well adapted not only to the soil and climate but to the
cultural conditions of hand ginning, hand spinning, and local marketing;
the foreign varieties, so much favoured by Lancashire, had to be cleaned by
a mechanical saw gin and so required a more complex technology than was
present in Indian culture at the time. The experimental farms on which
crops were grown without regard to expense were no models for cultivators
who lacked both the capital resources to experiment with unfamiliar
agricultural techniques and a clear motive for doing so.[2]

Despite the failure of the East India Company's cotton improvement
program, hopes of developing a new source of raw cotton in India
remained. This was one of the principal objects of the Cotton Supply
Association when it was formed in Manchester in 1857. The outbreak of
the American Civil War in 1861 provided the Association with a golden
opportunity to mount a campaign for renewed effort on the part of the
Government of India to turn India into a major supplier of good quality
cotton. As has been seen in chapter 2, the British Government – faced
with the threat of mass unemployment in England's most important
industry – was compelled to lend reluctant support to this campaign.

By 1863 the political pressure exerted by the Lancashire cotton lobby had
obliged the Secretary of State to sanction limited measures for improvement
of the quality of Indian cotton. Gradually, the scope of these measures
widened, aided by the fact that America was unable for some years after
the conclusion of the Civil War to resume cotton exports on the pre-war
scale. For about a decade after 1863, a large scale cotton improvement
program was again undertaken in India. Its objectives were to introduce
new and finer varieties of cotton suitable for manufacture in Lancashire,
to extend the cultivation of superior indigenous varieties, and to improve

[2]For a discussion of these and other points, see Seth Leacock and David G. Mandelbaum, "A Nineteenth Century Development Project in India: The Cotton Improvement
Program," *Economic Development and Cultural Change*, III (1955), pp. 334–41.

the staple and yield of existing varieties by modernizing traditional agricultural methods.

The attempt to introduce new varieties of cotton was concentrated on efforts to spread the use of the variety known as Dharwar American, which had been introduced into the Dharwar district of Bombay presidency by one of the American planters in the 1840s. This acclimatized New Orleans cotton had a longer and finer staple than Indian varieties and for a time its cultivation in Dharwar and adjoining districts spread. The Cotton Supply Association was anxious to see its cultivation extended to all parts of India. The Association's view was stated by its secretary, G. R. Haywood, who visited India in 1861–62. He wrote to the chairman of the Manchester Cotton Company from Dharwar expressing the belief that cotton improvement in India meant concentrating on the acclimatized plant: "Instead, therefore, of trying to improve the native, rather let attention be given to the improvement of the American, and there is ample black soil in India adapted to the growth of all that England or the Continent can possibly consume."[3] The Cotton Supply Association disliked hearing anything that cast doubt on this belief. For example, it criticized the Bombay Cotton Handbook, published in 1862 under the auspices of the Bombay government, because of its author's pessimism about India's ability to supply Great Britain with adequate quantities of superior cotton.[4] As a demonstration of its willingness to help, the Cotton Supply Association sent a circular to the India Office early in 1862 with its own suggestions for improving the quality of Indian cotton. Nine hundred copies of this circular were sent to India for distribution and translation into the vernacular languages.[5] The Association also forwarded to India for distribution by its agents in Bombay, Calcutta, and Madras a large number of samples of American-grown New Orleans cotton as examples of the kind of cotton Lancashire desired. In the following years, the India Office often acted as a post office for the transmission to India of samples of cotton seed obtained by the Cotton Supply Association from different parts of the world.[6]

[3]Haywood to Platt, 30 Nov. 1861. I. O., Rev. Dept., Home Corresp., Letters Rec., IV, no. 264. On his return to England, Haywood published a pamphlet entitled *India as a Source of the Supply of Cotton* (Manchester, 1862) in which he again sang the praises of Dharwar American cotton.

[4]*Cotton Supply Reporter*, 15 May 1862. For the Bombay Cotton Handbook, see above, p. 45.

[5]Cotton Supply Association to Secretary of State, 23 Apr. 1862. I. O., Home Corresp., Letters Rec., IV, no. 304.

[6]For example, Secretary of State to Government of Bombay, Despatch no. 5 (Revenue), 17 Feb. 1863; Under-Secretary of State to Cotton Supply Association, 26 Feb. 1864, requesting one ton of New Orleans seed for Madras. I. O., Home Corresp., Letters Sent, II, no. 237; *Report on the Administration of the Central Provinces for 1862–63* (Nagpur, 1863), para. 337, on results of efforts to cultivate Egyptian seed

Of much greater significance to Lancashire was the appointment by the Government of Bombay, with the concurrence of the Secretary of State, of the first official charged specifically with cotton-improvement work in India. This was Dr. G. F. Forbes, the former civil surgeon of Dharwar, who was appointed Cotton Commissioner of Bombay on 1 October 1863. Lancashire had long advocated the participation of British officials in the work of improving the quality of Indian cotton. There was a widespread belief among cotton manufacturers that the failure of the experiments conducted by the American planters in the 1840s was the result of sabotage on their part. The executive of the Cotton Supply Association was convinced that these experiments had not been fairly conducted.[7] The appointment of a British official would ensure that there would be no repetition of this. Moreover, Forbes was known to the Lancashire manufacturers, many of whom he had met while in England in 1860 purchasing machinery for the Bombay government's cotton gin factory at Dharwar, of which he was the superintendent. Forbes, indeed, was an enthusiastic propagandist for the Dharwar American cotton in which the Cotton Supply Association placed such faith, and as Cotton Commissioner he hoped to revolutionize Indian cotton production by introducing this variety into all parts of India.

But implementation of this policy required a change in traditional methods of cultivating and marketing cotton. Almost from the time when New Orleans seed was introduced into the Dharwar district in the 1840s it had become mixed with the indigenous variety known as Kumpta, the two sometimes being sown together and sometimes sown in separate fields but with the seed getting mixed in ginning. Often this was simply due to carelessness on the part of the cultivators, but frequently it was done deliberately. The reason was that the produce of almost every field sown with cotton was purchased in advance by *sowcars* (bankers) and speculators, who took a chance on being able to sell the cotton in the picking season at a price higher than when the contract was made in the sowing season. The speculators covered themselves from possible losses by mixing indigenous cotton brought in from neighbouring districts with the higher priced Dharwar American variety. The two kinds of cotton were cleaned together and the product sold as Dharwar American. The mixed seed was then returned to the ryots as part of the contract that kept them more or

supplied by the Cotton Supply Association. Many other examples are to be found in the Revenue Despatches to India, Madras, and Bombay.

[7]Speech by Hugh Mason at the third annual meeting of the Cotton Supply Association, 11 May 1860. *Cotton Supply Reporter*, 15 May 1860. Isaac Watts, who was secretary of the Association for most of its existence, subsequently admitted that the charges against the American planters were unfounded. Isaac Watts, *The Cotton Supply Association: Its Origins and Progress* (Manchester, 1871).

less permanently in the merchant's debt.[8] This practice became widespread during the American Civil War when rising cotton prices encouraged wild speculation. By 1865 it looked as though Dharwar American cotton, as a distinct variety, would be eliminated altogether. Forbes determined to take preventive action since his plan to spread this variety to other parts of India depended on the availability of adequate supplies of pure Dharwar American seed.

At first, Forbes hoped to secure such seed by persuading the ryots to alter their traditional methods of cultivation. He thought this could be achieved in one of two ways. He offered to purchase fields or portions of fields from the ryots, have the different varieties of cotton picked separately, reserve the Dharwar American seed for distribution during the next sowing season, and sell the cotton with the help of the Bombay merchants. Alternatively, he proposed to persuade the ryots to let him pick their New Orleans cotton separately from their other cotton, gin it, and return the cleaned cotton to them, while retaining the seed and paying the ryots for its value. Forbes toured the Dharwar district but found that the ryots did not favour his plan since for the time being only a few of them would profit from it. He thought the reason for their attitude was that the amount of money needed to implement the scheme was more than Rs 100,000 (£10,000) and the Bombay government had sanctioned only Rs 6,000 for the purpose. But it was also that the ryots preferred dealing with the local moneylender, a familiar figure in traditional society, to buying seed from a government official for whom they could conceive no social role and whose real purpose might be to increase taxes on their lands if the new crop was successful. Having failed to secure the cooperation of the cultivator, Forbes had to try a different tactic.

Since traditional marketing arrangements involved the wholesale disposal of the cotton crop to middlemen, Forbes decided he would work through them. The Bombay Cotton Frauds Act of 1863 provided penalties of up to twelve months' imprisonment and a fine of Rs 1,000 for persons adulterating cotton in any way, or selling such cotton (see chapter 6). He determined to use this legislation as a lever. He called together the dealers and *sowcars* in each of the various *taluks* (administrative subdivisions) of the Dharwar district and struck a bargain with them. His plan was to secure the first picking of Dharwar American cotton, which ripened two weeks before the indigenous variety and would be free of native seed. He would keep the seed from this cotton for the next sowing season, and since seed obtained from one acre of cotton was enough to plant sixteen acres of land, Forbes calculated that the produce of the

8G. F. Forbes to Government of Bombay, 27 May 1865, cited in *Cotton Supply Reporter*, 1 Sept. 1865.

first picking would be more than enough to secure all the seed he required. Forbes got the middlemen to enter into a written engagement to preserve carefully a sufficient quantity of the cotton first picked to supply the required seed, and to open depots during the sowing season from which the ryots would procure what they needed. In return for these pledges Forbes promised that cotton from the current season's crop, together with whatever stocks remained from the previous season, would be allowed to pass to Bombay without interference from the inspectors appointed under the Cotton Frauds Act. The dealers were left with the impression that if they did not do what Forbes wanted their cotton would be confiscated. As an additional inducement Forbes agreed to reimburse them out of the funds he had received from the Bombay government for any losses incurred in carting the seed to the depots and selling it there.

Forbes was pleased with the results of his efforts. He had required the dealers to issue receipts to the ryots for the quantity of seed sold to them These showed that 3,060 ryots had purchased 1,218,520 lb. of Dharwar American seed. After this was sown and the plants had grown sufficiently for the American and indigenous varieties to be distinguished, Forbes went on an extensive tour of the district and his observations, together with reports from the *mamlatdars* (subordinate Indian officials), convinced him that the native plant had been largely displaced. After the crop had been picked, Forbes toured the cleaning establishments and what he saw reinforced his belief that the mixing of the two varieties had been stopped.

Subsequent events showed that he was mistaken. It soon became clear to the dealers that the Bombay government, in keeping with instructions received from London and from the Government of India, had no intention of allowing its officers to interfere with traditional methods of agriculture by preventing a cultivator from mixing two varieties of cotton if he saw fit. Indeed, it had already warned its officials that in applying the Cotton Frauds Act – which Forbes had used to browbeat the Dharwar dealers – the greatest care must be taken to avoid interference with the free action of the ryots.[9] Without the coercive power of the government to support his efforts, Forbes's scheme failed and the ryots continued to mix the different varieties as before.

There was another reason for Forbes's failure. During the East India Company's cotton improvement program, as part of its effort to stimulate innovation in the agricultural sector, the Bombay government had set up a factory in 1847 to produce saw gins able to clean the new variety of cotton. This factory, of which Forbes was superintendent from 1855

9Bombay, Revenue Dept. Compilations, IX (1865), no. 592.

to 1863, charged fees for maintenance work on gins. But when the war in America ended and cotton prices fell, the cultivators and dealers were no longer willing to pay the necessary fees. The saw gins fell into disrepair and cultivators and dealers preferred to mix different varieties and clean them as best they could on the broken gins or grow indigenous varieties which could be cleaned by traditional methods, on the *churka* (hand-roller) or the foot-roller.[10]

There was still another explanation for the failure of the campaign to extend the cultivation of Dharwar American cotton. This came out clearly in the North-Western Provinces where the local government spent Rs 25,000 in the period 1864–67 on buying, shipping, and distributing Dharwar seed supplied by Forbes. It also published instructions in the vernacular for the guidance of cultivators and either sold the Dharwar seed at the same price as that of local seed or gave it away. But these efforts failed completely, since neither *zamindars* (landlords) nor cultivators were willing to undertake a new form of cultivation which involved much additional labour without any increased return and the risk of complete loss. They pointed out that the sowing season and methods of cultivation of Dharwar American which had to be planted in rows and not sown broadcast, were different from those for the local cotton, and they complained that often the seed did not fetch as good a price as the indigenous variety. Zamindars took the seed when it was free only reluctantly and either because they thought that by doing so they would please the government, or because they thought that they were complying with government orders.[11] After three years of negative results, the local government abandoned the experiment.

Hopes that Dharwar American cotton would be the means of revolutionizing Indian cotton cultivation, already dimmed by these failures, were further reduced as a result of extensive tests of this variety carried out in 1871–72 and 1874–75. The tests were sponsored jointly by the India Office, the Cotton Supply Association, and the Society of Arts and were carried out in both Manchester and India. The results led the Director of the Indian Museum in London to conclude that Dharwar American had preserved the characteristics of its prototype in only one respect: of all the varieties of cotton grown in India it was freest from leaf. But, regarding the staple of the cotton, the acclimatized plant had deteriorated considerably. The staple was shorter and the fibre was strongly attached to the seed.

[10]Report by G. F. Forbes on the Cotton Crop of the Southern Division, Bombay Presidency, for 1867–68 dated 8 May 1868. Bombay, Rev. Dept. Comp., V (1868), no. 988.

[11]Government of North-Western Provinces to Government of India, no. 176, 13 Feb. 1868. India, Revenue Proceedings, XXV (1868), 15 Feb. 1868, nos. 29–30, and 21 Mar. 1868, nos. 27–28.

It was inferior in strength and evenness of fibre and in length of staple to the indigenous Kumpta cotton.[12]

Throughout the 1870s the cultivation of Dharwar American continued to decline, even in the Dharwar district itself where the success initially achieved in introducing it had been partly due to the blandishments of government officials. Forbes admitted that in such matters the influence of the Collectors increased the farther they were from Bombay and the legalistic atmosphere which prevailed in the provincial capital. According to Forbes, this was why in 1847 the Collector of Dharwar had been able to induce the ryots to grow Dharwar American cotton in the first place.[13] Similarly, his own retirement from government service in 1872 removed much of the drive behind the effort to extend the cultivation of this kind of cotton throughout the Bombay presidency and to other parts of India.

Experimental cultivation of other foreign varieties had no better success in this period. In the Central Provinces, to cite only one example, an acclimatized type of American cotton known as Upland Georgian was introduced on a small scale. But, like the Dharwar American in Bombay, it did not remain in its pure state and quickly became one of the constituents of the mixed cotton of the region.[14]

The failure with Dharwar American came as no surprise to those, from the Governor of Bombay down, who argued that the best way to improve Indian cotton cultivation was to concentrate on indigenous varieties.[15] Even Lancashire finally came to accept this view.[16] Accordingly, for several years a strenuous effort was made both in Bombay presidency and in the Central Provinces to spread the cultivation of superior Indian cottons.

In Bombay the effort centred on Khandesh district where the Collector, Lionel Ashburner, tried to displace the coarse Deshi cotton traditionally grown there with the finer cottons of neighbouring Berar and the Central Provinces. His methods resembled those of Forbes in Dharwar in that he used his official position to persuade the ryots to change their traditional methods of cultivation. To start with, he seized the opportunity provided by the drastic fall in cotton prices which occurred when the American war ended in 1865. Cotton cultivation fell from 465,534 acres to 237,911

12The tests were carried out to determine the best saw gin for cleaning Dharwar American cotton. The results were published some years later by John Forbes Watson, *Report on Cotton Gins and on the Cleaning and Quality of Indian Cotton,* 2 vols. (London, 1879), I, p. 30.

13Bombay, Rev. Dept. Comp., XIII (1869), no. 701.

14D. N. Mehta, "Cotton Breeding in the Central Provinces and Berar," in Indian Central Cotton Committee, *First Conference of Scientific Research Workers on Cotton in India* (Bombay, 1938), pp. 402–403.

15Minute by Sir Seymour Fitzgerald, Governor of Bombay, 10 Jan. 1868. Bombay, Rev. Dept. Comp., VIII (1869), no. 90.

16Watts, op. cit., p. 22.

acres, and in 1865–66 Ashburner was able to import enough Amraoti (Oomrawutti) seed from Berar to sow most of the reduced acreage under cultivation in Khandesh. In fact, he claimed that only 18,131 acres were planted with the variety indigenous to his district and most of this was planted with Gowranj cotton, which was very similar to the Berar variety. He purchased the seed of the small remaining acreage under Deshi cotton to sell in Bombay as cattle food.[17]

Ashburner claimed that careful experiments showed the Amraoti cotton yielded an average of 186 lb. of uncleaned cotton per acre, which gave 62 lb. of cotton when cleaned. This compared with an average of 150 lb. of uncleaned and 50 lb. of cleaned cotton for the Deshi variety. He also argued that the new cotton was more easily and quickly cleaned by the churka than the old. Still another advantage, in his view, was the fact that Amraoti cotton ripened later, thus permitting the ryot to harvest his grain crop before cotton picking demanded every available labourer.

In 1867, Ashburner reported triumphantly the entire elimination of the cotton hitherto grown in Khandesh. Only one small field of less than three-quarters of an acre had been sown with the old seed and he took steps to destroy the seed produced from this field. The seed sown in 1866–67 was that produced in the previous season from the imported Amraoti seed. Ashburner claimed that despite a partial failure of the monsoon in part of his district the gross yield per acre of the improved crop had increased by 18 per cent and that of clean cotton by 14 per cent.[18]

Not satisfied with these results, the enthusiastic Ashburner next decided to displace the Amraoti cotton after only two years by an even better variety known as Hingunghat from the Central Provinces. This he did on a small scale in the 1867–68 season, restricting operations to two or three taluks where enough Hingunghat cotton was grown to supply the entire district in 1868–69. Ashburner stated that the ryots were so anxious to cultivate the new variety that in one taluk they had even offered to send a deputation to Hingunghat to buy the necessary seed. But Ashburner refused to permit this, partly because he feared that any sudden demand would push seed prices up, and even more because he feared that the result would be the cultivation of two varieties in the same fields with consequent deterioration in quality.

For a time it looked as though Ashburner's efforts were succeeding, but in 1872 he left Khandesh and the momentum behind his campaign disappeared. The ryots, freed from the pressure of the district officer, soon began to revert to the indigenous variety. They did so because the

17L. R. Ashburner to Revenue Commissioner, Northern Division, no. 456, 17 Mar. 1866. India, Rev. Procs., XXIII (1866), 24 Apr. 1866, no. 13.
18Ibid., no. 369, 18 Feb. 1867. India, Rve. Procs., XXIV (1867), 12 Apr. 1867, no. 13.

innovations desired by Ashburner – who saw himself as a modernizer attempting to bring about productive changes in traditional agriculture – ran counter to forces in the traditional society which had their own logic behind them and which he and his successors failed to perceive.

In the first place, both ryots and middlemen preferred the indigenous cotton because it produced a large crop in normal times and a fair crop in seasons of deficient or excessive rainfall. Hence it was more profitable even though its price was slightly lower than the longer-stapled varieties from Berar and the Central Provinces. Moreover, even though Lancashire did not want it, there was demand for it in certain European countries and in the cotton mills of Bombay.[19] As the Bombay Chamber of Commerce itself admitted, as long as that demand continued, merchants would buy it, middlemen would mix it, and cultivators would grow it.[20]

Secondly, the ryots of Khandesh – like those of Dharwar – lacked the capital to retain a portion of their crop for use as seed the following season. Their crop was usually mortgaged to the local moneylender and they procured their seed from him just before the beginning of the sowing season against seed to be delivered after the crop was gathered. This had two implications. One was that the seed so procured was a mixture of different varieties because it came from both early and late pickings – in which there was a wide difference in quality – and because it was mixed by pickers who were paid in kind for their labour and who naturally took no trouble to keep the different varieties separate before selling their share to a dealer. The other implication was that the decision as to what kind of cotton should be planted rested with the dealers and moneylenders and not with the ryots. In the case of Hingunghat cotton, its long silkiness was marred by the presence of leaf in the fibre and since appearance was an important factor in determining the value of cotton, some *baniyas* (traders) conceived the idea of importing coarse cotton to mix with the Hingunghat to give it a better colour. This led to reintroduction of Deshi seed which, despite Ashburner's optimistic claims, had not been completely eliminated. The ryots found to their surprise that because the production of Deshi was limited at first, they could get even more for this coarse cotton to be used for adulteration than for the more valuable Hingunghat staple. Naturally, they at once recommenced sowing it. The baniyas adulterated the Hingunghat gradually, each year adding more and more coarse cotton. The price of Khandesh cotton then began to fall but the old cotton continued to spread; the seeds mixed in ginning were sown together, until

[19]Memorandum by the Director of Land Records and Agriculture, Bombay, 9 Mar. 1889. Bombay, Rev. Dept. Comp., LXXXVIII (1889), no. 847.

[20]Bombay Chamber of Commerce to Government of Bombay, 15 Jan. 1885. Bombay, Rev. Dept. Comp., LXXVII (1885), no. 18.

finally there was no more pure Hingunghat seed to be had in Khandesh.[21]

When the authorities realized that the ryots of Khandesh were reverting to Deshi cotton, the Bombay government – with the full approval of the Government of India and the India Office in London – ordered the Collector of Khandesh to use his utmost influence to discourage this development. The Collector, W. H. Propert, had some success at first but the ryots soon discovered that his orders could not be legally enforced. Propert's explanation of his failure to check the growth of Deshi cotton shows the changing attitude of the people to government authority and the growing awareness of their rights:

> In the days when Mr. Ashburner so successfully stamped out the indigenous cotton, it was far easier in a province such as Khandesh for the Executive Head of the District to take strong measures, although unsupported by any special legal enactment, than at the present time. The people now are, comparatively speaking, conversant with our laws, and as they know that I cannot force them to abstain from sowing Deshi cotton, they quietly and gradually do as they think best.[22]

In other words, the modernizing force of British legal institutions could be called into play to counter the modernizing activities of innovating officials attempting to interfere with a set of market calculations embedded in the traditional sector. This was clearly brought out when Propert, in response to pressure from his superiors, published a general notification in English and Marathi for distribution in every village in effect ordering the ryots to abstain from growing Deshi cotton. This produced an immediate reaction in the vernacular press. The *Khandesh Vaibhav* commented that the government was saying to the producers that since they habitually mixed inferior and superior kinds of cotton, they should not sow inferior cotton at all. It criticized Propert's orders as unnecessary and uncalled for and said that if people chose to mix two varieties of cotton and offer them for sale, the government had no right to interfere.[23] This alarmed the Government of India, which feared political difficulties. But in fact, the ryots paid no attention to Propert's orders and in some cases actually told his assistants that in future they would grow whatever cotton they pleased.

Efforts to improve cotton cultivation by spreading the use of superior indigenous varieties had no better success in other parts of India. In the

[21]Memorandum by H. E. M. James, Rev. Commr., N. Div. Bombay, Rev. Dept. Comp., XCVII (1891), no. 814 (I).

[22]Collector of Khandesh to Rev. Commr., C. Div., no. 1706, 31 Mar. 1882. Bombay, Rev. Dept. Comp., LI (1882), no. 849.

[23]*Report on Native Newspapers Published in Bombay Presidency and Berar*, week ending 29 Apr. 1882.

Central Provinces, a Cotton Commissioner was appointed in 1866 in response to the "strong feeling in Lancashire that the appointment of such an officer would greatly promote the growth of cotton and the improvement of the mode of cultivation of the plant grown."[24] The man appointed to the new post was J. H. Rivett-Carnac, a young Indian Civil Service officer whose previous experience was in land revenue work. He took office on 1 September 1866 with instructions to improve cotton cultivation; to improve the process of picking, cleaning, and packing cotton for the market; and to perfect arrangements for the transport of cotton to the coast.[25]

The main task Rivett-Carnac set himself was to check the process whereby the local cotton, Hingunghat (which Ashburner was trying to introduce into Khandesh), was being displaced in the Central Provinces by coarse Deshi cotton from Khandesh. The reason for this was that although Hingunghat was the best of all Indian cottons in terms of strength and length of staple it had certain defects. One was the presence of leaf in the fibre. Apart from that, it ripened later than Deshi cotton, was not so hardy, and was more difficult to pick. Also its ginning capacity was low – the proportion of wool to seed rarely exceeded 26 per cent – and this was the most important factor accounting for its replacement by another variety.[26] Again, there was an economic explanation.

Both cultivators and middlemen in the Central Provinces had compelling reasons to prefer the coarser variety: the ryots because it was easier to grow, ripened earlier, and was easier to pick; the middlemen because of its higher ginning percentage (33 per cent); and the merchants because of the demand for it in some European countries and from the growing Bombay mill industry.[27] Some European cotton mills had machinery specially designed to spin this type of cotton, and access to this market became easier with the opening of the Suez Canal in 1869.[28] Such factors were not taken into account either by those in Lancashire who still hoped that they could obtain Indian cotton that would compete with American, or by British officials intent upon imposing English ideas on Indians without regard to Indian economic and social conditions.

Not only did Rivett-Carnac fail to check the disappearance of Hingunghat cotton in the Central Provinces where it became one of the constituents

---

[24]Earl de Grey, Secretary of State for India, to Sir John Lawrence, 19 Mar. 1866. John Lawrence Collection, Letters from the Secretary of State, III, no. 15.

[25]*Report on the Administration of the Central Provinces, 1866–1867* (Nagpur, 1867), para. 188.

[26]Mehta, op. cit., p. 402.

[27]*Report of the Indian Cotton Committee* (Calcutta, 1919), para. 74.

[28]This point was made in the Bombay Legislative Council by A. H. Campbell, the representative of the European mercantile community, during a debate on Cotton Frauds legislation in February 1869, Bombay, *Legislative Council Proceedings*, VIII, p. 51, 17 Feb. 1869. See also ch. 6, following.

of the mixed cotton of the region; but he also failed in his efforts to spread
its cultivation to other parts of India. The reaction in Madras was typical.
One district officer in that province begged the local government not to
send him Hingunghat seed because the ryots preferred the indigenous
cotton of their region.[29] But the Madras government, aware of the
importance attached to the effort by the authorities in England, persisted
in distributing large quantities of seed sent from the Central Provinces.
The results were negative and prompted the Board of Revenue to protest
at "the futile character of these random attempts to improve agriculture
by the occasional issue of good and bad seed, ill-understood agricultural
exhibitions and the like."[30]

Efforts to improve cotton cultivation in India by introducing new
varieties and extending the cultivation of existing varieties were mainly
the work of officials such as Forbes, Ashburner, and Rivett-Carnac,
who were appointed, or encouraged in their efforts, in order to appease
Lancashire. At the same time, attempts were being made to improve the
staple and yield of Indian varieties by improving traditional methods of
cultivation and by careful seed selection. These efforts centred on
experimental farms set up for the purpose, under the direction of seed
gardeners recruited from the Royal Botanical Gardens at Kew. The plan
was potentially a good one since yields per acre of Indian cotton were
exceedingly low, averaging in the best districts perhaps 50–60 lb. of clean
cotton per acre compared with an average yield of 160 lb. per acre in
the United States.[31]

The first seed gardener, William Shearer, was appointed in 1866.
Before he arrived in Bombay, a proposal was made to carry out a systematic

[29]Madras, Revenue Dept. Proceedings, 5 Nov. 1867, no. 587.

[30]Ibid., 5 Nov. 1870, nos. 580–581.

[31]Accurate figures of output per acre for India do not exist but during the American
Civil War, when the question of cotton supply to England was an urgent one, the
authorities in India made a determined effort to find out yields per acre. These varied
greatly, even within a limited area. In the Central Provinces, the range was from 20–80
lb. of clean cotton per acre, and the average was taken to be 50–60 lb. in Nagpur
district and 40–45 lb. elsewhere; in Bombay, the Acting Cotton Commissioner estimated
in 1867 that the average was 60 lb. for Dharwar American and 43 lb. for indigenous
varieties, whereas ten years later the average yield per acre for both kinds was estimated
at 48 lb. per acre. See *Report on the Administration of the Central Provinces, 1866–1867*,
para. 187; India, Rev. Procs., XXIV (1867), no. 12; and *Administration Report of the
Bombay Cotton Department for 1875–1876* (Bombay, 1876). On the other hand, an
unofficial but careful compilation of Indian cotton statistics published in 1889 considered
that yields per acre were often estimated too low. This source provides alternative
estimates for each cotton-growing region and revises the all-India average upward from
the official estimate of 54 lb. per acre to 71.8 lb. per acre. See A.F.B., *Statistical Tables
Relating to Indian Cotton* (Bombay, 1889), pp. 20–23. For American output, see U.S.
Bureau of the Census, *Statistical History of the United Stated States from Colonial Times
to the Present Day* (Stamford, Conn.: Fairfield Publishers; distributed by Horizon Press,
New York, 1965), Table K83–97.

analysis of the soils of Western India to serve as a guide for him. No such analysis had ever been made despite years of unsuccessful cotton experiments. But when the chemical analyst to the government stated that this would take at least a year, even if only forty samples were submitted, the plan was dropped. Lancashire was clamouring for results and the government wanted to waste no time. So Shearer had to spend his first year in India getting used to the country and finding out about Indian methods of cotton cultivation. Then, in June 1867, Forbes rented eleven acres of land near Dharwar where Shearer could begin work.

From the outset, the experimental farms ran into difficulties over financing, organization, and administration. For his first year of operations, Shearer received a grant of only Rs 1,000 (£100). In addition to lack of funds, he faced the skepticism of Forbes, who believed that whatever success might have been achieved in England by the system of seed selection, in India the utmost effort of the government would not be sufficient to provide enough gardens for the purpose of selecting superior seed. All Forbes expected from the effort to improve cotton by the selection of seed under trained English gardeners was encouragement to the ryots to follow the example by themselves selecting their seed more carefully.[32]

After a year, Forbes moved Shearer to the other end of the Bombay presidency to carry on his work in Gujarat. He also secured the appointment of three more gardeners, one to assist Shearer and the others to work in Khandesh and Sind. The Cotton Supply Association was asked to nominate a fourth, but declined.[33] But funds to support their activities were always insufficient and in 1872 the Bombay government would have closed down the farms but for an emergency appropriation from the Government of India.[34] Because of the lack of funds to purchase land outright, the gardeners — whose titles had been changed in 1869 to "Superintendents of Experimental Farms" — merely rented fields here and there from the ryots and gave them up at the end of the season. In effect, the "farms" existed only in name. Even the funds that were available were uncertain. For example, at the Khandesh experimental farm the grant was sometimes Rs 2,000 a month for a few months; then it would suddenly be withdrawn. Monthly grants not fully expended lapsed. Funds were often not available at the critical sowing season. Such bureaucratic bungling made it impossible for the superintendents to plan ahead.[35]

[32]Forbes to Rev. Commr., S. Div., no. 110, 16 July 1868. Bombay, Rev. Dept. Comp., V (1868) no. 874.

[33]Secretary of State to Government of India, Despatch no. 86 (Revenue), 11 Nov. 1869.

[34]Bombay, Rev. Dept. Comp., X (1872) nos. 578 and 1100.

[35]Rev. Commr., N. Div. to Government of Bombay, no. 2189, 8 May 1873. Bombay, Rev. Dept. Comp. XXVI (1874), no. 497. Ashburner, who wrote this report, drew on his experience as Collector of Khandesh. He pointed out that in 1869–70, only one year

As an economy measure, the government decided in 1873 to abolish the post of Cotton Commissioner and put the superintendents directly under the Collectors; it also directed that in future all farms must "pay their way." This system was even worse. In 1873–74 the Khandesh farm had only 371 acres under cultivation and no less than 40 different products, including cotton, were grown. This procedure was then criticized by the government, which argued that the main object of the farms was to improve native agriculture rather than to experiment with many different crops.[36] It therefore directed the superintendents to concentrate their efforts on instructing the ryots to adopt well-tested agricultural methods, spreading the use of Hingunghat cotton, and raising seed for sale to the cultivators. But as the superintendent of the Khandesh farm drily remarked, in the matter of making the best of their own crops, the European farmer was able to teach the ryots very little. "Having myself been instructed by them in the first place in such details, it is not surprising that they do not consult us concerning the sowing of their jowari and bajri."[37]

Meantime, the government continued to starve the farms of funds, thereby seriously restricting their operations. In 1873 the superintendent at Surat had so little to do that he was employed as a part-time inspector under the Cotton Frauds Act. The rest of his time he spent observing the ryots, getting to know them, and trying out implements. The superintendent at Dharwar was reported to have had no work to do for twelve months.[38] Three years later the reports on the experimental farms were even more critical. At Surat little or nothing had been done during the year for lack of funds and in May 1876 the farm was closed. At Dharwar, few agricultural experiments worth the name had been attempted and in October 1877 that farm was also closed. The results at Khandesh were considered slight compared with expenditure, modest though this was; and the government remarked with heavy humour that the model farm in Sind "was not a model of success."[39]

In the Central Provinces the story of failure was much the same, only shorter lived. In 1870 four seed gardeners were appointed to this province to work under the direction of the Cotton Commissioner, Rivett-Carnac. When he gave up this post in the following year to become Commissioner

after the farm was started, orders were received just as the sowing season commenced to stop all expenditure except what was necessary to save the standing crop. Then in 1870–71, Rs 24,000 had been granted. A similar sum was put into the budget for the following year but was cut in half just when it was urgently required and afterwards increased at a time when it was useless. In 1872–73, Rs 15,000 was originally provided but then cut to Rs 12,000.

[36]Bombay, Rev. Dept. Comp., XXVII (1875), no. 1124.
[37]*Report of the Bombay Cotton Dept., 1875–1876*, p. 78.
[38]Bombay, Rev. Dept. Comp., X (1873), no. 815.
[39]Ibid., XXX (1876), nos. 1098 and 1865; XXXVIII (1877), no. 1283.

of Cotton and Commerce with the Government of India, the provincial cotton department ceased to exist and the three seed farms which had been established in the Central Provinces – at Hingunghat, Amraoti, and Khangaon – were put directly under the local government. Two of the farms were abolished in 1873 on the ground that the experiments carried on in them had not succeeded and that ryots would not adopt "improved" methods of agriculture until it had been proved that they could produce a better crop by such methods.[40]

In the North-Western Provinces, model farms were established in 1870 at Cawnpore and Allahabad under the direction of seed gardeners recruited from Kew. Over the next few years, the desultory efforts made on these farms – again, only land rented from zamindars – to introduce both foreign varieties and indigenous cottons from other parts of India completely failed.

By 1872 it was becoming clear that the experimental farms were not producing satisfactory results anywhere in India. The whole cotton improvement program then came under critical review when the Central Provinces government complained to the Government of India that the experimental farms established in its territory in 1869–70 were an object of ridicule to the ryots. The Government referred this complaint to W. S. Halsey, the acting Commissioner of Cotton and Commerce. Halsey's lengthy report on the experimental farms clearly exposed the reasons for their failure.[41]

First, the experimental farms had been started and operated without any distinct or definite principle. Some of the men who were sent out from England to act as superintendents thought their task was to teach the ryots the rudiments of agriculture. Instead of being told to study the native system of husbandry and find out in what ways it could be improved, they had simply assumed that the Indian cultivator was absolutely ignorant and had everything to learn. Through ignorance of India, and of Indian agricultural methods, the farms had never been able to produce crops equal to those of the Indian cultivator. In the selection of seeds, the trained gardeners had failed entirely. All that the experiments had demonstrated to the ryots was purposeless extravagance, an example they were hardly likely to follow.

Second, the experimental farms had been badly managed. Experiments in the truest sense had never really been tried because every year the land

[40]"Historical Account of the Efforts Made to Grow Long-Stapled Cotton in India," IV, Central Provinces and Berar, in *Notes Prepared for the Indian Cotton Committee* (no place or date; volume is in University of British Columbia Library).
[41]Report by W. S. Halsey, Officiating Commissioner of Cotton and Commerce, on Experimental Farms, 30 Sept. 1872. India, Rev., Agric., and Commerce Proceedings, November 1874, nos. 1–5.

on which experiments were made was changed. Moreover, in every case, either of starting a farm or changing a site, it was never done until just as the sowing season was commencing. The unfortunate superintendents had therefore to contend with the overwhelming disadvantage of unprepared land and a farm without buildings, implements, or stock.

Halsey believed that the proper approach to agricultural development in India was not to try to introduce English methods of husbandry but to try to improve on existing methods. He argued that the ryot had only to be shown how to grow anything in a more profitable form – in a way that would produce definite results – and he would soon adopt it. He cited several examples to support his argument. During the Crimean War the Indian cultivator had responded to the demand in Europe for oil seed, and during the American Civil War he had responded to the demand for cotton. He had seen the advantages of cultivating maize and sugarcane. For several years at Cawnpore, where Halsey was Collector, the whole of the experimental farm's crop of maize had been sold or stolen for seed purposes. Yet large quantities of cotton seed had been distributed free and had not been wanted. In the one case the cultivator knew the value of what he was buying or stealing, and in the other he had no faith. "Depend on it," concluded Halsey, "the cultivator of the country and his friend, the moneylender, are keenly alive to their interests, and ready to adopt any change which results in a quick practical return."[42] But such change would have to be practical and economical for the ryot lived a hand-to-mouth existence and could not afford to run risks – the seasons alone were a sufficient risk.

Halsey's critical assessment of the results of the cotton improvement program was not a solitary one. From an independent source – John Forbes Watson, the Director of the Indian Museum in London – came supporting evidence. In his report on the cotton gin trials of 1871–72 and 1874–75, Watson considered the subjects of improvements in the selection of seed and cotton cultivation generally. He concluded that no perceptible progress had been made despite fifty years of effort and he attributed this in large measure to bureaucratic bungling in the operation of the experimental farms.[43] Watson also poured cold water on the idea that quick results could be achieved by selection of seed and by improved cultivation, manuring, and irrigation. The plan was simple in theory, but such methods required years of well-directed effort to produce successful results. In addition, he criticized the policy of carrying on a program of cotton improvement in isolation from the broader problem of agricultural improvement.[44]

[42]Ibid.
[43]Watson, op. cit., I, p. 30.
[44]Ibid., II, p. 196.

A similar conclusion was reached by William Walton, who had been for many years an inspector on the staff of the Bombay cotton department. He had once been an enthusiastic proponent of the cotton improvement program. Early in 1867, while acting as Cotton Commissioner of Bombay during Forbes's absence in England, Walton reported optimistically on the "great strides" that were being made in the improvement of cotton in India.[45] But in 1880, in an article written for the official *Bombay Gazetteer*, he remarked sadly on how little use was ever made of the valuable experience so often gained as a result of experimental cultivation. Often, the commonest laws and principles of nature were ignorantly set aside; one experimenter took no notice of what another had done and so committed the same mistakes and got the same results, announcing them as new while the record showed that what had been done had been done repeatedly before.[46]

By 1872, when Halsey wrote his report, the impetus behind the program had died down. In England, the Cotton Supply Association disbanded that year and one of the main forces behind the program disappeared with it. Lancashire by this time was as dependent on the United States for the bulk of her cotton supplies as before the Civil War, and there seemed little point in continuing to press for the development of India as an alternative source of cotton. In India, where the authorities had never given wholehearted support to the program, the posts of Cotton Commissioner were abolished: in the Central Provinces in 1871 and in Bombay in 1873. Two years later the post of Commissioner of Cotton and Commerce with the Government of India was abolished. The Department of Revenue, Agriculture, and Commerce, which had been set up in 1871, after a lengthy campaign by the Cotton Supply Association, to improve and develop agriculture, commerce, and industry in India was also abolished as an economy measure.[47] The experimental farms were mostly wound up in the same period.

Thus the second cotton improvement program of the nineteenth century failed as its predecessor of the 1840s had failed before it. In explaining the reasons for failure, the emphasis differs for the different areas of innovation. Attempts to introduce new varieties of cotton and to spread the cultivation of selected indigenous varieties failed mainly because such attempts were made without sufficient botanical knowledge or the necessary market research. The cultivation and marketing of existing varieties produced a

[45]W. Walton, Acting Cotton Commissioner, to Rev. Commr., N. Div., no. 279, 28 Feb. 1867. India, Rev. Procs., XXIV (1867), 12 Apr. 1867, no. 12.

[46]W. Walton, *A Short History of Cotton, its Culture, Trade and Manufacture in the Belgaum and Kaladgi Districts of the Bombay Presidency* (Bombay, 1880), p. 69.

[47]Arthur W. Silver, *Manchester Men and Indian Cotton, 1847–1872* (Manchester: Manchester University Press, 1966), pp. 279–85.

relatively stable and acceptable rate of return to ryots, moneylenders, and dealers. New and untested varieties involved different methods of cultivation and greater labour input, without a higher level of output and profit, and with the risk of severe loss to each of these classes. Attempts to improve the staple and yield of indigenous varieties failed principally because those involved did not perceive that agricultural development involved both theoretical knowledge, in which they were deficient, and perception of the intricate patterns of village life and of the economic relationships that derived from them. Moreover, the innovators did not have the sustained administrative and financial support of government in this period.

Finally, the cotton improvement program failed because of its basic misconception. It was geared to the needs and interests of English industry, not to the interests of India. It was designed to provide a resource desired by Lancashire manufacturers who themselves were unwilling to make technological or market adjustments in their industry which would have made Indian cotton more acceptable to them. Most of them produced the higher counts of yarns and piece goods aimed mainly at the quality export and domestic markets. For this, the short-stapled Indian cotton was unsuitable. But it found an expanding market in India itself, where the number of cotton mills was increasing rapidly, and in continental Europe and Japan, where much of the machinery had been constructed for spinning low and coarse counts of yarn and cloth. In the 1870s, Lancashire resumed her former dependence on the United States for the bulk of her cotton supplies and lost interest in India as an alternative source. The cotton improvement program, which was a direct response to Lancashire's earlier hopes of India, was accordingly wound up. At the same time, another aspect of the cotton improvement program – the attempt to improve the quality of Indian cotton by legislative action to prevent its adulteration – also came under critical review.

6

THE STATE AND COTTON IMPROVEMENT
Legislative Aspects, 1863–82

"I DON'T THINK A BILL would go down here for punishing mixture of Native with American cotton," remarked Sir Charles Wood to the Governor of Bombay in 1863, adding: "I have no faith in extraordinary measures for remedying evils which are of a permanent character."[1] His statement, provoked by a bill then before the Bombay Legislative Council to curb the adulteration of cotton, epitomizes a debate that was to last for almost the next two decades over the role the state should play in preventing frauds in the cotton trade with a view to improving the quality of Indian cotton. The poor quality of Indian cotton, as compared with American cotton, made it highly unpopular in Lancashire. The problem was due in part to the character of the Indian cotton plant and the previous chapter has described the measures taken in India in the mid-nineteenth century in an attempt to make Indian cotton more acceptable to Lancashire. But low quality was due even more to adulteration of the cotton after it was picked and cleaned. This occurred because cotton in India was bought and sold by weight and changed hands many times on its way from the cultivator to the ship on which it was loaded for export. Each of the many intermediaries involved in the cotton trade was therefore

---

[1] Wood to Frere, 18 Mar. 1863. Halifax Collection, India Office, Letter Books, XII, pp. 140–41.

tempted to adulterate the cotton in order to increase the profit from its sale. Thus, they exposed it to the night air so that it would absorb the dew; they added rubbish, stones, and other material to the bales of loosely packed cotton; and they mixed inferior quality cotton with superior varieties.

Legislation to control such practices had been passed in 1829 and 1851 but had proved ineffective. This was because the authorities in India, under pressure from Lancashire to increase cotton cultivation, were reluctant to take any action which might have an adverse effect. The deterioration of Dharwar American cotton because of the admixture of native varieties has already been described but the government was unwilling to intervene for fear that this would discourage cultivation of the superior variety. For this reason, in 1859 the Bombay government rejected a proposal from the Bombay Chamber of Commerce that district officers should be given the power to compel the peasant not to grow more than one variety.[2] Two years later it terminated the practice whereby police officers at Broach and Surat examined about ten per cent of the cotton bales exported to Bombay to ensure that they were free from stones and rubbish. When the Bombay Chamber of Commerce protested, the government replied that serious complications would arise if it undertook to examine bales of cotton and trade marks. It feared that it might then be called on to do the same for wool, linseed, and other products, something that it considered ought to be done, if at all, by the merchants themselves. Such a view was fully in keeping with the principles of free trade.

But the outbreak of war in America, and the consequent rise in the price of cotton, made the inducement to adulterate stronger and the practice more widespread. A section of the Bombay mercantile community, looking beyond the immediate export boom to the prospect of developing a permanent trade, and sharing the belief of the Manchester Cotton Supply Association that this was a practical possibility, began to demand government intervention to control the situation.[3] In September 1862 the chairman of the Bombay Chamber of Commerce asked leave in the Bombay

[2]Bombay, Revenue Dept. Compilations., LIV (1859), no. 582.

[3]There were close ties between the commercial interests of Lancashire and Bombay. For example, Walter R. Cassels of the Bombay firm of Peel, Cassels, and Company, which represented the Cotton Supply Association in India, was a prominent member of the Bombay Chamber of Commerce, author of the Bombay Cotton Handbook (1862), and a member of the Bombay Legislative Council from 1863 to 1865. Andrew Cassels, another partner in this firm, was a member of the Board of Directors of the Manchester Chamber of Commerce until 1868; in 1874 he was appointed as Lancashire's first representative on the Secretary of State's Council. Similarly, Samuel Smith, who founded the Liverpool cotton-broking firm of Smith, Edwards, and Company, became a partner in the Liverpool branch of the Bombay firm of James Finlay and Company. He was president of the Liverpool Chamber of Commerce and also represented Liverpool in Parliament.

Legislative Council to introduce a bill for the suppression of fraud in the cotton trade. At the same time, the Chamber complained to the Bombay government about the increase in adulteration which had followed the ending of police supervision at Broach. It proposed the appointment of a commission to look into the whole matter. The government agreed and in October appointed a commission, three of whose seven members were nominated by the Chamber of Commerce.

The commission presented its report in January 1863. It stressed the growth of the practice of adulteration in its various forms since the outbreak of the American war and called for fresh legislation to remedy the evil. But how could such a demand be reconciled with free trade principles? The commission took a purely pragmatic view:

> We are strongly impressed with the belief, that as a general rule it is not judicious to interfere by legislative enactment in matters connected with trade, but looking to the circumstances of the present case, to the growing extent and to the dangerous nature of the frauds, to the immense importance of the question at the present time as affecting not only local, but national, interests, and to the apparent inefficiency of the present law, we are forced to the conviction that exceptional and more stringent legislation is necessary.[4]

The commission drafted a bill to implement its recommendations and it was introduced into the Bombay Legislative Council by Michael Scott, the chairman of the Bombay Chamber of Commerce, on 31 January 1863. It provided penalties of up to twelve months' imprisonment and a fine of Rs 1,000 (£100) for persons adulterating cotton in any way, or for selling adulterated cotton, or for having it in one's possession. Mere possession would be considered as evidence of intent to sell. The bill also provided for the licensing of all establishments packing, pressing, and screwing cotton.

When the bill came up for debate in the Legislative Council, one of the government-appointed official members, A. D. Robertson, led the opposition. His argument, which had been made repeatedly in the House of Commons by Sir Charles Wood, was grounded in *laissez-faire*, for there was "no principle in the economy of trade more certain in its operation than that prices adjust themselves to the supply of the demand both as regards quality and quantity."[5] Robertson accused Bombay merchants of knowingly buying and shipping adulterated cotton to England for fear that if they rejected it, the seller would ship it on his own account and they would lose business. Other opponents of the bill claimed that its penal provisions were inconsistent with the recently enacted Indian Penal Code. The bill was accordingly referred to a select committee which removed the

[4]*Report of the Cotton Frauds Commission*, p. 8, encl. in Frere to Wood, 12 Feb. 1863. Halifax Collection, India Office, Correspondence, India.
[5]Bombay, *Legislative Council Proceedings*, 31 Jan. 1863, II, Part I, p. 87.

provision that mere possession of adulterated cotton was evidence of intent to sell it. Thus amended it passed into law as Act IX of 1863. In order to ensure enforcement, the Act created an inspecting establishment and imposed a levy of four annas (about 6d) a bale to pay for it on cotton exported from Bombay.

One of the most significant aspects of this legislation is that it did not emanate from the government. It was framed, introduced into the Legislative Council, and conducted through all its stages by the chairman of the Chamber of Commerce. It was opposed by some official members and the Governor of Bombay, Sir Bartle Frere, assented to it after much hesitation. In forwarding it to the Governor-General for his assent, Frere explained that while most Bombay merchants, both European and Indian, were in favour of some such measure, there was much difference of opinion over certain of its provisions.[6]

The reluctance of the government and the division in the ranks of the Bombay merchants led to great caution in implementing the Act, for this was the first attempt at state interference in India in the fields of production, marketing, and trade. The Chamber of Commerce informed the government that most merchants thought the authorities should confine themselves to a very gentle exercise of the powers conferred by the law. Some merchants resented the fact that the Chamber's chairman had played such a prominent role in securing passage of the legislation because this gave the impression that he was acting in his official capacity. They asked the Chamber not to express any corporate opinion on the question of implementation.[7] Scott's own view, which he had earlier expressed in the Bombay Legislative Council, was that the mere existence of such legislation, and the machinery to enforce it, would be a sufficient deterrent to adulteration. It was generally agreed that the inspectors appointed to implement the Act would have to be chosen with great care.

The Bombay government accordingly drew up rules which varied from district to district to suit the varying operations of the cotton trade and which were purposely vague. Chief emphasis was placed on the port of Bombay from which most of the cotton exported to Europe was shipped. A staff of European inspectors and Indian assistants was appointed and assigned the duty of visiting the cotton pressing establishments in the districts. They were also instructed to obtain information on the quality of cotton being packed at the presses.[8] The government ordered the

[6]Government of India to Secretary, Bengal Chamber of Commerce, no. 64, 13 Feb. 1868. Bengal, Revenue Dept. Proceedings, May 1868, no. 4.

[7]Bombay Chamber of Commerce to Government of Bombay, 7 Dec. 1863, no. 129. India, Revenue Consultations, XLIX (1864), 17 Feb. 1864, no. 4.

[8]Extract from the Proceedings of the Government of Bombay in the Revenue Department, 12 Dec. 1863. India, Revenue Consultations, XLIX (1864), 17 Feb. 1864, no. 4.

inspectors to be tactful in dealing with the merchants and cultivators but to be vigorous in prosecuting cases of deliberate fraud, orders which proved difficult to carry out.

For the first three years after the Cotton Frauds Act went into force on 1 January 1864 it seems to have worked effectively.[9] In England, the Cotton Supply Association claimed that the quality of Indian cotton now made it acceptable to fully one-half of Lancashire's spindles and looms.[10] But almost from the outset complaints came from the Bombay Chamber of Commerce. It admitted that one form of adulteration had diminished: the addition of rubbish to bales of cotton. But the Act had not prevented the mixing of two or more different varieties of cotton. More vigorous intervention by the state would have been necessary to meet this objection; but the Bombay government, supported by the Government of India, argued that the Cotton Frauds Act was designed only to prevent fraudulent and dishonest mixtures, such as adding uncleaned cotton, seed, or dirt to clean cotton. It did not think that the law should prevent a cultivator from mixing two varieties of cotton if he saw fit.[11] Another complaint was over the levy of four annas a bale on exported cotton in order to meet the expenses of the inspecting establishment. This appeared irksome when cotton prices fell at the end of the American war. Here the government was able to give some relief and it reduced the levy from four to three annas in May 1865.[12] To meet complaints about the mixing of different varieties of cotton, the inspector-in-chief of the cotton frauds department suggested using some of the funds at his disposal to pay informers to report on which cultivators were doing it. This proposal, which implied a considerable degree of state interference, was turned down by the government. It did, however, authorize the inspectors to try and persuade the cultivators to use improved varieties of cotton seed and better methods of cultivation.

In authorizing the inspectors to engage in such activities, the government warned that the greatest care must be taken to avoid interference with the free action of the ryots.[13] Even so, this represented a shift in emphasis from using the Cotton Frauds Act as a punitive weapon to prevent adulteration to employing it as an instrument for agricultural improvement. The government asked for the opinion of the Chamber of Commerce on this matter and suggested an increase in the export levy to the former level

[9]Frere to Wood, 7 June 1864. Halifax Collection, I. O., Corresp., India; Government of Bombay to Secretary of State, Letters nos. 20, 15, and 17 (Revenue), 28 Mar. 1865, 8 June 1866, and 24 May 1867 respectively.
[10]*Cotton Supply Reporter*, 1 July 1865.
[11]India, Revenue Consultations, XLIX (1864), 17 Feb. 1864, no. 4.
[12]*Report of the Bombay Chamber of Commerce for 1864–65*, p. 312.
[13]Bombay, Rev. Dept. Comp., IX (1864), no. 592

of four annas a bale to provide funds for cotton improvement work.[14] The Chamber's reply revealed the growing opposition in the Bombay mercantile community to such legislation: it agreed that the quality of Indian cotton had improved since the Act had gone into force but argued that the reasons lay elsewhere. Chief among these were the fall in world prices, which meant that Indian cotton again had to compete with American, and the opening of rail communications with the interior, which brought merchant and cultivator into direct contact and led to the establishment of European agencies at the main cotton marts and to the introduction of machinery for cleaning and pressing cotton at these places. A considerable section of commercial opinion in Bombay, believing such legislation useless in practice and wrong in principle, wanted the Act repealed. But the majority wanted it retained for its deterrent effect and supported the proposed use of part of the cotton frauds fund for improvement work without, however, any increase in the export levy.[15] Indeed, there was general agreement that the levy should be reduced and eventually abolished. In other words, most Bombay merchants were prepared at this stage to support the principle of agricultural improvement but they were not prepared to subsidize it.

Meanwhile, a proposal had come from the cotton commissioner of the Central Provinces and Berar, Harry Rivett-Carnac, to extend the Bombay Cotton Frauds Act to these territories. This would involve the creation of an additional inspection agency and Rivett-Carnac claimed a subsidy of Rs 70,000 from the Bombay cotton frauds fund to support it. He argued that the completion of the railway through Berar to Nagpur in the Central Provinces had led to the establishment of pressing companies at various places along the line. Cotton pressed in these places needed to be examined before being exported to Bombay in order to prevent adulteration. Rivett-Carnac also proposed that the inspectors should play the same role in cotton improvement work as the inspecting staff in Bombay. The Bombay government accepted these proposals in principle but was advised by its solicitor that the law did not permit the expenditure of Bombay funds beyond the limits of the presidency.[16] For Rivett-Carnac's scheme to be implemented, the Government of India would have to pass enabling legislation. Thus what had been a purely provincial matter up to 1867 became one which involved the Indian and Home Governments.

At first, the Government of India was willing to pass the necessary legislation and it introduced a bill into the Supreme Legislative Council

---

[14]India, Home Dept. (Revenue) Proceedings, 19 Nov. 1867, no. 1.

[15]Bombay Chamber of Commerce to Government of Bombay, Home Dept. (Revenue) Proceedings, 12 Aug. 1867, no. 116.

[16]Bombay, Rev. Dept. Comp., VIII (1867), no. 625.

in August 1867.[17] It was sympathetic to the idea because the previous March it had been asked by the Bengal Chamber of Commerce to take action to prevent the widespread adulteration of cotton in the North-Western Provinces and the local government had agreed that legislative action was required.[18] Moreover, opinion in England at this time was favourable to general legislation to check the adulteration of cotton, since the American cotton trade had not yet recovered from the dislocation caused by the Civil War. The Chambers of Commerce of Manchester and Liverpool expressed satisfaction at the improvement in the quality of Indian cotton which had resulted from the Bombay legislation of 1863, and the India Office, under the Conservative Sir Stafford Northcote, was interested. For the British government, the question of an improved supply of cotton was still one of "imperial concern" and the Secretary of State for India was even willing to sanction an increase in the export fee on cotton in order to provide an adequate inspectorate.[19]

But strong mercantile opposition to more extended legislation began to develop in India. The Bombay Chamber of Commerce disliked the proposal to transfer legislative control from the provincial to the supreme government which, being more remote, was less amenable to its influence. And it was still convinced that the improvement in the quality of Indian cotton was not due primarily to the Cotton Frauds Act.[20] To the Bombay merchants, the tax on exports levied under the Cotton Frauds Act amounted to giving an unfair advantage to America in the renewed competition for the English market. As merchants, their interests were confined to trade; they did not extend to the wider issues of agricultural development in India. The Madras Chamber of Commerce also opposed legislative action by the Government of India, although one local firm engaged in the cotton trade strongly supported the idea.[21] Finally, a prominent Calcutta firm, Gladstone, Wyllie, and Company, which was extensively engaged in the cotton trade, vigorously protested to the Government of India against its threatened interference in commercial affairs, and in particular against the "unusual and hateful system of espionage on the business of private individuals."[22] This firm declared it

17India, Home Dept. (Legislative) Proceedings, August 1867, no. 27.
18Government of North-Western Provinces to Government of India, 25 Sept. 1867, no. 923A. Ibid., November 1867, nos. 3-6.
19Secretary of State to Government of Bombay, Despatch no. 60 (Revenue), 14 Sept. 1867. The Government of India also favoured an increase in the export levy because the cotton frauds fund had incurred a deficit of Rs 34,000 in 1866-67. This deficit was more than covered by the large surpluses accumulated in the two previous years.
20Bombay Chamber of Commerce to Government of Bombay, 18 Feb. 1868. India, Home Dept. (Legislative) Proceedings, March 1868, nos. 9 and 10.
21Madras Chamber of Commerce to Government of Madras, 1 Oct. 1867. India, Home Dept. (Legislative) Proceedings, December 1867, no. 4.
22Messrs. Gladstone, Wyllie, and Co. to Government of India, 27 Jan. 1868. India, Home Dept. (Legislative) Proceedings, February 1868, no. 14.

would give up its cotton presses rather than be subject to the kind of interference proposed.

Faced with such widespread opposition, the Government of India hesitated. It asked the Bengal Chamber of Commerce if the views expressed by Gladstone, Wyllie, and Company represented commercial opinion generally in Bengal and was told that they did not.[23] Next, it asked the opinion of several of the provincial governments on the proposed imperial legislation.[24] It received mixed replies. The North-Western Provinces retreated from its earlier support for such legislation and asked instead for the appointment of a Cotton Commissioner whose task would be to distribute cotton seed, promote the use of the best kinds of cotton cleaning and pressing machinery, and conduct experimental cotton cultivation. Bombay, ever jealous of its prerogatives as a presidency government, was opposed to imperial legislation to check cotton frauds. It wanted only an enabling Act to permit it to transfer a portion of its cotton frauds fund to the cotton commissioners for Bombay and the Central Provinces to enable them to carry on improvement work. Bengal and the Central Provinces, on the other hand, strognly supported legislative action by the Government of India.[25]

The Government of India itself was divided on the best course of action. Two members of the Governor-General's Council – Mansfield, the Commander-in-Chief, and Massey, the Finance Member – favoured imperial legislation because they considered that the export fee collected in Bombay on all cotton passing through the port, regardless of its point of origin, was really a transit duty. Moreover, the funds raised in this fashion were spent exclusively in Bombay presidency. An imperial Act would permit the Government of India to distribute such funds among all provinces that contributed cotton exports. There was also a feeling of

---

[23]Bengal Chamber of Commerce to Government of India, 20 Mar. 1868. India, Home Dept. (Legislative) Proceedings, March 1868, no. 17.

[24]Government of India to Governments of Bombay, Bengal, Central Provinces, and North-Western Provinces, 23 Apr. 1868. India, Home Dept. (Legislative) Proceedings, August 1868, nos. 17–20.

[25]Government of North-Western Provinces to Government of India, 8 May 1868, no. 606; Government of Bombay to Government of India, 14 Sept. 1868, no. 130P; Government of Bengal to Government of India, 5 Aug. 1868, no. 356T; and Government of Central Provinces to Government of India, 11 Sept. 1868, no. 2947–288; in India, Home Dept. (Legislative) Proceedings, August 1868, nos. 21–24, and November 1868, nos. 4–6. Rivett-Carnac accused the Bombay cotton commissioner, G. F. Forbes, of circulating the rumour that the proposed imperial legislation "was a dodge of the '*Bengal Government*' to take all the patronage out of the hands of the Governor and to put it in Bengal people, and the Bombay people took alarm and were quite ready to make out of it a Bombay versus Bengal question." Rivett-Carnac to Richard Temple, n.d. Richard Temple Collection, 56 (Letters from Civil Officers, Central Provinces, 1862–67).

resentment in the supreme government arising from the fact that the cotton frauds fund was the only one in India over which it had no legal control. On the other hand, Maine, the Law Member, considered that the Bombay government had much more experience in carrying out such legislation than the Government of India, and he believed that it should not be interfered with.[26] The upshot was that the supreme government decided not to go ahead with its legislation; instead, it asked the Bombay government to amend its Act to permit the transfer of part of the proceeds of the cotton frauds fund to the Central Provinces.[27]

The Bombay government complied and introduced the necessary bill into the Legislative Council in February 1869. It was designed to tighten the existing law relating to cotton frauds, permit the expenditure of funds raised by the export levy on cotton improvement, and allow the transfer of part of these funds to the Central Provinces. The bill ran into strong opposition. A. H. Campbell, speaking as representative of the European commercial community in Bombay, opposed the expenditure of money on cotton improvement. He claimed that Lancashire was not seeking a greatly improved staple from India. Everybody knew that, given the state of Indian agriculture, this was expecting the impossible. Lancashire only required cotton of a uniform quality, although Campbell pointed out that despite the outcry from British manufacturers concerning the quality of Indian cotton, half the cotton exported from India went to continental Europe from which no complaints were received.[28] The representative of the Indian merchants, Munguldass Nuthoobhoy, opposed the bill for a different reason. He complained that native importers of Lancashire piece goods suffered heavy losses from the frauds extensively and systematically practised by Manchester manufacturers who mixed clay, sand, and other matter in sizing piece goods in order to increase their weight and improve their appearance. His point was that if laws were necessary to protect the interests of British manufacturers, there should also be legislation

[26]Maine to Sir John Lawrence, 25 Sept. 1868. John Lawrence Collection, XII, no. 144.

[27]Lawrence to Sir Seymour Fitzgerald (Governor of Bombay), 25 Sept. 1868. John Lawrence Collection, XXV, no. 50.

[28]Much of the textile industry in countries like Italy and Austria-Hungary was geared to producing low quality coarse cloth for which the short-stapled Indian cotton was quite suitable. The spinning machinery was designed to work with such cotton. The opening of the Suez Canal in 1869 brought the consumer and supplier into direct contact, where hitherto much of the Indian cotton exported to continental Europe had been in the form of re-export from England. See memorandum by H. E. M. James, Commissioner in Sind, 7 July 1891, no. 2351. Bombay, Revenue Dept. Compilations, XLVII (1891), no. 814. Of course, the cotton manufacturers of foreign countries were not in a position to complain or to influence British policy in India, as the Lancashire manufacturers were.

to protect Indian merchants, traders, and consumers.[29] In other words, from the point of view of the Indian business elite, Indian interests should not be subordinate to those of commercial groups in Britain.

One of the main points of contention was whether it should be illegal to mix different varieties of cotton. The bill had a provision to that effect which was deleted in select committee but restored when the bill again came before the Legislative Council in September 1869. It was included in the bill as passed. The opponents of the measure then took their case to the Government of India. Both the Bombay Chamber of Commerce and the Bombay Association sent petitions to the Governor-General protesting against such legislation as unnecessary, unenforceable, and open to abuse.[30] The Bombay Association claimed that the bill was directed against Indians and would not be applied against Europeans.[31] Such a claim was an indication that the conflict over cotton frauds legislation was stimulating the incipient nationalism of the emerging business elites in Bombay.

When the bill came before the Governor-General for his assent in December 1869 it encountered severe opposition in his council. John Strachey used such epithets as "thoroughly discreditable" and "monstrous" to describe it and the Law Member, J. F. Stephen, was also scathing in his condemnation. Mayo accordingly decided to exercise his veto.[32] Opinion in Lancashire was also cool by now. The Manchester Chamber of Commerce raised several objections, the chief of which was that the stiffer penalties provided under the new law were too harsh and might discourage cultivation of cotton. It also believed the legislation would be ineffective since it applied only to Bombay, and not to Madras and Bengal.[33] The Liverpool East India Association agreed and asked the Secretary of State to use his veto if the Governor-General refused to disallow the bill.

Thus the new Bombay legislation, itself a substitute for an imperial enactment, was defeated. To its opponents it represented an increasing degree of state intervention in private trade which was distasteful to them. The Bombay merchants disliked – though for different reasons – the system

[29]Bombay, *Legislative Council Proceedings*, 17 Feb. 1869, VIII, pp. 44–51. This is an important early example of nascent Indian mercantile opinion expressing its opposition to special legislation designed to suit the interests of British merchants. It was to become more vocal when the Indian cotton manufacturers of Bombay organized themselves into the Bombay Millioners' Association in 1875 in order to counter Lancashire pressure in Parliament. For confirmation of the complaints of the Indian merchants, see R. A. Arnold, *The History of the Cotton Famine* (London: Saunders, Otley 1864), p. 513.

[30]India, Legislative Proceedings, May 1870, nos. 2–19.

[31]Bombay, *Legislative Council Proceedings*, 17 Feb. 1869, VIII, p. 51.

[32]India, Legislative Proceedings, May 1870, nos. 2–19 ("Keep-With" Notes by Strachey and Stephen).

[33]*Proceedings of the Manchester Chamber of Commerce* (Manchester Central Reference Library), vol. 7 (1867–72), 23 Feb. 1870.

of inspection already in force which would have become even more irksome under the stiffer provisions of the new law. This was related to the fear that, given India's social conditions, such a system would be open to abuse and might thus discourage cotton cultivation, to the detriment of the export trade. The Bombay government's answer to such objections was that the legislation adopted in 1863 had not discouraged cotton cultivation and the new bill had not been aimed at the cultivator in any case, but at the middlemen who handled the cotton on its way from the grower to the port of export.[34] But these arguments went unheeded. To mercantile opposition in both Bombay and Lancashire must be added the hostility of influential members of the Government of India who objected to the legislation because of their belief in the principles of *laissez-faire* and who also resented the independence enjoyed by the Bombay government in the disbursement of the cotton frauds fund.

The veto of the bill of 1869 left the original Act of 1863 still in force. It also left the question of assisting the cotton improvement program in the Central Provinces up in the air. In October 1870 the Government of India sanctioned the appointment of six additional seed gardeners for the Central and North-Western Provinces; they augmented the existing staff of four gardeners who had been appointed earlier to work in Bombay. The cost of these new appointments was charged to the Bombay cotton improvement fund, the source of which was the fee levied on cotton exported from Bombay. Four months later, in February 1871, Rivett-Carnac submitted a budget of Rs 48,750 to support his cotton improvement operations for the ensuing fiscal year. This created a new conflict within the Government of India. The Finance Department approved this budget, but the Home Department refused to ask the Bombay government to pay over the money on the ground that the law did not permit this. Enabling legislation would first have to be passed before such payments could be made.[35]

Before the question of new legislation could be tackled, the Bombay merchants launched a further attack on the legislation already in force. This time they employed different tactics. In March 1871 the Bombay Chamber of Commerce sent a petition to the Bombay government protesting that the Cotton Frauds Act made a crime of certain acts connected with a particular trade (the mixing of different varieties of cotton) that were not in themselves criminal. To reinforce this new line of approach the Chamber repeated the familiar objections: that the Act put a tax on the cotton trade to support the inspecting agency; that it

[34]Sir Seymour Fitzgerald to the Duke of Argyll, 28 Jan. 1870. Argyll Papers (India Office Library, microfilm reel no. 319).
[35]India, Legislative Proceedings, June 1871, nos. 66–69.

had been passed in exceptional circumstances which no longer existed; and that it did nothing to prevent the mixing of different varieties of cotton.[36] The Bombay government referred this petition to the Inspector-in-Chief of the Cotton Department, but his voluminous reply was not ready until May 1872.[37] By then, the balance against the legislation had been tilted considerably by the decision of the Government of India to press for its repeal. It did so because it considered such legislation undesirable in principle and a possible source of oppression. It was prepared to accept gradual abolition of the inspection system and meanwhile asked the Bombay government to reduce the export fee to two annas a bale.[38]

This decision by the Government of India, coupled with the appointment of a new Governor of Bombay, Sir Philip Wodehouse, in May 1872 led to a detailed re-examination of the whole question of cotton frauds legislation by the Bombay government.[39] While this was in progress the Bombay Chamber of Commerce kept up its pressure and on 7 January 1873 seemed to have won its case following an interview between a deputation of merchants and the Governor. For Wodehouse wrote to the Viceroy on the same day:

> Until this afternoon I think I would have said that we were in favour of retaining the Cotton Frauds Act and the establishment, the latter very much reduced, for another year at any rate; but this afternoon I had a long talk with a deputation from the Chamber of Commerce who protested that the Act was perfectly useless, that they were taxed for nothing, and that in the existing condition of the Cotton trade, dealers were perfectly able to take care of themselves.[40]

Before finally making up his mind, Wodehouse decided to consult mercantile opinion in Britain and he asked the Chambers of Commerce of London, Glasgow, Liverpool, and Manchester to state their views – a typical example of the way in which British commercial interests were given the chance to influence the course of Indian policy. The first two did not

[36]Bombay, Rev. Dept. Comp., X (1872), no. 824.

[37]A. T. Moore, *Indian Cotton, Its Adulteration and Acts Passed to Suppress the Same* (Bombay, 1872).

[38]Government of India to Government of Bombay, 25 Jan. 1872, no. 28. Bombay, Rev. Dept. Comp., X (1872), no. 824. The Government of India had recently set up the new Department of Agriculture, Revenue, and Commerce with A. O. Hume as secretary. Hume was a doctrinaire supporter of *laissez-faire*. At a higher level, John Strachey and James Fitzjames Stephen were members of the Governor-General's Council and were firm holders of *laissez-faire* principles. The Bombay government reduced the levy as requested on 16 May 1872.

[39]Ibid., IX (1873), no. 358.

[40]Wodehouse to Northbrook, 7 Jan. 1873. Northbrook Collection (India Office Library, MSS, Eur. C. 144/14).

reply. The Manchester Chamber split on what to do. A sub-committee of six directors took four heated meetings to discuss the matter. Eventually, three directors came out in favour of retaining the legislation, two were opposed, and one abstained. Their discussion showed that many Manchester manufacturers and Liverpool cotton brokers supported legislation because of the improvement in the quality of Indian cotton which had taken place since 1863. There had also been widespread complaints of the scandalous adulteration of American cotton during the previous year. But when the matter came before a full meeting of the directors of the Chamber, the opponents of state intervention carried a resolution (by 12 votes to 7) declaring that the improved quality of Indian cotton was due in some measure to the natural operations of trade and to the improvement of communications in India. Consequently, the Manchester Chamber of Commerce told the Bombay government that it was not prepared to recommend absolute repeal and asked for such modifications in the existing law as the government thought necessary from its own knowledge of the situation.[41]

Given this uncertainty in Lancashire, the Bombay government postponed a final decision on whether or not to repeal the Cotton Frauds Act. It had already met the Government of India's request for a reduction in the export fee. In August 1873 it passed legislation to legalize payments which had been made from the cotton frauds fund since 1865 for cotton improvement work. Then, in March 1874, it appointed a commission to look into the whole question of cotton frauds legislation. The commission took nine months to report and was not unanimous in its findings. Two of its three members recommended suspending the Act on grounds both of economic principle, which ruled out state interference in matters of trade, and of the practical difficulties of enforcement, since no statute could define what kind or degree of adulteration justified state intervention.[42] The government decided to accept the majority view, and on 30 June 1875, it announced its intention to suspend the Act and disband the inspection force.

At this point, the Secretary of State, Lord Salisbury, intervened. He

[41] *Proceedings of the Manchester Chamber of Commerce*, vol. 8 (1872–79), 26 Mar. 1873. Manchester was obviously torn between its theoretical adherence to the principles of *laissez-faire*, which precluded interference by the state in matters of trade, and its practical desire to see India emerge as an effective competitor with America, which required legislative and administrative action on the part of the Indian government to bring about an improvement in the quality of Indian cotton. Its action at this time represents a compromise between the two points of view. See also Arthur Redford, *Manchester Merchants and Foreign Trade*, 2 vols. (Manchester: Manchester University Press, 1934 and 1956), II, p. 20.

[42] Report of the Commission ... with Minutes of Evidence, 12 Jan. 1875. Bombay, Rev. Dept. Comp., XXVII (1875), no. 501–I.

telegraphed instructions to Bombay halting any action and followed this with a despatch explaining the reason. The feeling at the India Office was that mere suspension of the Act, instead of total repeal, showed lack of confidence in the policy of abandoning the safeguards which the law provided. Salisbury ordered the Bombay government to amend those sections of the Act which had proved too harsh, and to amend it further to make the law more effective.[43] The Bombay government, rebuffed by London, prepared to obey but came in for strong opposition from the local commercial community. A meeting of merchants, both European and Indian, called a public meeting for 11 September 1875 to protest retention of the Act and the export fee.[44] The meeting drew up a memorial to this effect and sent it to London. But the Secretary of State rejected it and bluntly ordered the Bombay government to carry out his previous instructions.[45] He thus clearly revealed in this as in his peremptory actions over the tariff, discussed in chapter 2, where the ultimate decision-making power rested in Indian affairs.

The necessary legislation was introduced into the Bombay Legislative Council in October 1876 and was passed by it in the following March. The main change it made in the Act of 1863 was that adulterated cotton was liable to confiscation but persons who had committed the act were not otherwise punishable. Hitherto, persons convicted of adulterating cotton had been liable to imprisonment, or fine, or both. Another feature was the provision that the government might apply fees and fines levied under the authority of the legislation to the promotion and improvement of cotton cultivation.

The passage of this measure provoked a storm of protest from the local merchants which was not assuaged by the decision of the Bombay government to abolish the post of inspector-in-chief of the Cotton Department as an economy measure from 1 September 1877. Another public meeting of Bombay merchants was held on 20 April 1877. This one drew up a memorial to the Governor-General which asked him to veto the legislation, even though it had been passed at the instance of the Home

[43]Secretary of State to Government of Bombay, Despatch no. 10 (Revenue), 27 May 1875. The continuing division in both Bombay and Manchester is shown by a letter written by a Bombay merchant named Voy to the Manchester Chamber of Commerce urging it to support retention of the Act. Two directors proposed that the Chamber should do so but two opponents moved the previous question and this was carried. *Proceedings of the Manchester Chamber of Commerce*, 28 Apr. 1875. A note on the draft despatch to Bombay shows that Salisbury himself was doubtful of the wisdom of retaining the legislation and more inclined to leave the cotton trade to the operation of "natural agencies." But his Council was in favour of the despatch as sent.

[44]Encl. in Government of Bombay to Secretary of State, Letter no. 34 (Revenue), 25 Oct. 1875.

[45]Secretary of State to Government of Bombay, Despatch no. 5 (Revenue), 27 Jan. 1876.

government, and which protested against state interference in matters of trade. The Chambers of Commerce of Manchester and Liverpool, preparing for an attack in Parliament on the Indian cotton duties, now gave support by sending similar memorials to the India Office.[46] There was also strong opposition in the Governor-General's Council and the Viceroy himself, Lord Lytton, considered such legislation "altogether an anachronism." He wanted it repealed and received strong backing from Sir John Strachey, a long-time opponent of state intervention, and other members of his council.[47] The Government of India accordingly asked London for further instructions and Lytton withheld assent to the legislation in the meantime. But the India Office was still not convinced that repeal was desirable. The former inspector-in-chief had prepared a long memorandum defending government action to prevent frauds in the cotton trade; the Secretary of State sent it to the Governments of India and Bombay in January 1878. Soon after, the Manchester Chamber of Commerce sent a deputation to the India Office to complain that legislation did not prevent frauds but harassed trade and put weapons into the hands of government officials which they often misused. Salisbury promised that Manchester's views would be given "great weight" in reaching a final decision.[48]

The decision was taken by Lytton, who decided to veto the Bombay bill despite a protest from the Governor of Bombay. As a compromise, the Government of India said it would accept an amended version of the bill with the provision for a cotton improvement fund omitted. The Government of Bombay thereupon passed an amended version of its bill in 1878 which received the Governor-General's assent in November of that year (as Act VII of 1878).[49]

The response of the commercial interests to this development was not long delayed. The first reaction came from Manchester. The Chamber of Commerce, on the verge of successfully concluding its long campaign to secure abolition of the Indian cotton duties on the ground that they hampered free trade, could hardly justify state intervention to promote agricultural development in India at the same time. Moreover, it had lost its interest in India as a source of raw cotton. It therefore sent another deputation to the India Office in February 1879 and followed this with a memorial later in the month. This was sent to the Government of India

[46]*Proceedings of the Manchester Chamber of Commerce*, 25 Apr. 1877; India, Home, Revenue, and Agriculture Proceedings, September 1879, no. 67. On 10 July 1877 the House of Commons passed a motion proposed by the Manchester members of Parliament Jacob Bright and Hugh Birley, calling for outright repeal of the cotton duties (see above, p. 33).

[47]India, Legislative Proceedings, September 1878, nos. 1–14 ("Keep-With" Note by Sir J. Arbuthnott, Lord Lytton, and Sir J. Strachey).

[48]*Proceedings of the Manchester Chamber of Commerce*, 27 Mar. 1878.

[49]India, Legislative Proceedings, November 1878, nos. 4–10.

without comment.[50] Next, the Bombay Chamber of Commerce sent in its protest. The Bombay government remained firm in its support of the legislation, pointing out that Manchester was not the only market involved in measures designed to improve the quality and reputation of Indian cotton, but the Government of India was equally firm in its opposition. As one of its secretaries, C. E. Bernard, noted in a revealing comment on a draft letter in the Home, Revenue, and Agriculture Department: "It is difficult to conceive a stronger case for interposition with the decision of a Local Government now that the English consumers have turned against the Act."[51] This reached the heart of the matter: British mercantile opinion did not want the legislation; therefore it must be repealed. The Government of India enlarged on this theme in explaining its attitude to the Home Government. It had accepted Act VII of 1878 for no other reason than that there seemed to be some uncertainty about the attitude towards it on the part of the chief English dealers in Indian cotton. But now that it was clear that commercial opinion in Bombay and England was squarely against such legislation it must be repealed.[52] Could there be any clearer statement of the forces governing British legislative and administrative policy in Indian economic matters than this?

The Government of India strengthened its case by underlining certain anomalies in the law. Chief among these was the fact that the export fee was levied on cotton which came full-pressed to Bombay from the Central Provinces, Berar, and various native states. Such cotton could not be inspected by the cotton frauds department; in 1878 it had amounted to 400,000 of the 741,000 bales exported from Bombay. The remedy, of course, would have been imperial legislation along the lines proposed by the Government of India in 1867, when opinion in Lancashire, at least, was still receptive to the idea. But the Government had retreated under pressure from the merchants of Bombay and Madras; ten years later Lancashire was pressing for repeal of the Indian cotton duties and felt unable to support state intervention in another sector of the cotton trade, and the Government of India was controlled by men dominated by *laissez-faire* ideas. This is illustrated by the arguments put forward by the Government of India in September 1879 in pressing the case for repeal. It attacked the export fee as an objectionable form of taxation and employed all the familiar arguments of the free traders. A tax on any article must be defended in the interests of the revenue or because it

---

[50]*Proceedings of the Manchester Chamber of Commerce*, 3 Feb. 1879; Secretary of State to Government of India, Despatch no. 11 (Separate Revenue), 3 Apr. 1879.

[51]India, Home, Revenue, and Agriculture Proceedings, Sept. 1879, nos. 66–72 ("Keep-With" Note by C. E. Bernard).

[52]Government of India to Secretary of State, Letter no. 13 (Revenue), 15 Sept. 1879.

maintained some special institution for the general benefit. But on neither ground could the export levy be justified:

> The case is altogether different when the tax really falls on the producer, as this must check production and *pro tanto* diminish wealth. In order that the trade may throw this tax on the consumer, it is necessary that all of the goods of the sort taxed must pay at an equal rate; if some quantities of a given commodity are untaxed and others taxed, the holders of the latter, being forced by competition to sell at equal rates, cannot recover from the purchaser what they have paid as tax. Now in the present case some of our Indian cottons are taxed and others untaxed; both have to compete with the superior American cottons for the market; no one alleges that the consumer pays; the tax must either fall on the Bombay merchant, or, as the better opinion is, on the producer, who must dispose of his cotton for his livelihood, and thus must in the last resort take the rates the Bombay merchants are prepared to give him.[53]

Similar arguments had been used by Laing in justifying the reduction of the Indian cotton duties in 1862.[54]

Thus the arguments of classical economy could be used to show that the Indian peasants' interests were threatened. That the interests of the merchants were also being sacrificed on account of this deviation from sound economic principles was purportedly shown by the declining export figures, which are shown in Table 6.1.

Table 6.1

Exports of Raw Cotton from Bombay, 1874–75 to 1877–78

Year	Exports (cwt)	Av. Value per cwt (Rs)
1874–75	5,600,086	27.2
1875–76	5,009,788	26.5
1876–77	4,557,914	25.7
1877–78	3,459,077	27.1

SOURCE: Government of India to Secretary of State, Letter no. 13 (Revenue), 15 Sept. 1879.

Although it could not seriously be argued that the export fee – which since 1872 had been two annas a bale or less than .005d per lb. – was responsible for this decline, to the Government of India it afforded yet another reason for asking the Secretary of State either to disallow the Bombay Act of 1878 or to order the Bombay government to repeal it. It

53Ibid.
54See earlier, p. 26.

supported this request by the reminder that "weighty opinion" in Bombay, Liverpool, and Manchester was against it.

Surprisingly, in view of this powerful line-up of commercial interests along with the Government of India, the Conservative Secretary of State, now Lord Cranbrook, refused to give way. Indeed, he rejected the argument that in trade matters the state should not interfere to protect experts, that is, merchants who knew their own business: "The argument, in fact, as regards the statement of the case which it involves, is misleading. The object of special legislation has not been to protect experts, or to protect any individuals, but to guard the country from the misfortune of losing one of its most valuable export trades."[55] This, of course, was why legislation had been passed in 1863. Opponents of the legislation met this argument by claiming that the nature of the cotton trade had changed since then and that honest dealing had become more advantageous than fraud. The Secretary of State replied that this was opinion only, untested by experience, and that it was refuted by the Bombay government which predicted renewed adulteration if the legislation was repealed. Cranbrook admitted a weighty argument against the existing law was that it subjected all cotton exported from Bombay to a fee, regardless of its point of origin. This particularly irked the Bombay merchants. Lancashire disliked another aspect of the law, namely, that the growing Indian mill industry obtained whatever benefit the legislation conferred in the way of better quality cotton but did not have to pay any fee on the raw material it consumed. Cranbrook did not deny this either. But neither of these objections meant that special legislation against frauds in the cotton trade was unnecessary or mischievous. For such legislation had been in force for more than fifty years and was acknowledged by the highest mercantile opinion in both England and India to have stopped the worst frauds in the cotton trade. Even in America a system of voluntary supervision had been found necessary to guard against fraud.

The conclusion that the Secretary of State reached after this examination of the arguments for and against special legislation was that the best course would be to revert to the system in force before the passage of Act IX of 1863. This would mean disbanding the inspection establishment and abolishing the export fee but retaining the penal provisions against fraud and adulteration. On this basis the Bombay government received orders to repeal Act VII of 1878 and to restore the legislation of 1863 modified along the lines laid down.[56] Once more the Bombay Legislative Council carried out its instructions but by the time it did so Cranbrook was no

[55]Secretary of State to Government of India, Despatch no. 24 (Revenue), 4 Mar. 1880.

[56]Secretary of State to Government of Bombay, Despatch no. 16 (Revenue), 14 Mar. 1880.

longer in office, a new Liberal government having come to power in England.

The return of the Gladstone administration in 1880 encouraged the Government of India to reopen the whole case with a view to securing total repeal of all cotton frauds legislation. Assent was withheld from the latest Bombay bill pending a further reference to London.[57] The Government of India justified its action by referring to the unanimous opposition of the mercantile members of the Bombay Legislative Council and pointing to the fact that the bill had only passed by the votes of the official majority, although this was an equally common occurrence in the Supreme Legislative Council. This time it got its way. The new Liberal Secretary of State, Hartington, ordered the Bombay government to repeal all special legislation relating to cotton frauds and that government reluctantly obeyed in a bill consisting of only nine words, which passed the Legislative Council on 22 February 1882.[58]

Thus ended the long battle to improve the quality of Indian cotton by legislative means. The sequel was that predicted by the Bombay government. Within two years, the Liverpool Chamber of Commerce was calling for special legislation to check the adulteration of cotton which had revived as soon as the deterrent was removed. It declared quite erroneous the view held almost unanimously by the mercantile community in 1882 that the decline in adulteration since 1863 was due not to the special legislation but to the direct contact which had been established between growers and buyers as a result of improved communications.[59] The Manchester Chamber of Commerce agreed that adulteration had revived and it held several meetings in 1884 to consider what should be done about it. But it reached deadlock over a proposal to join the Liverpool Chamber in demanding special legislation. Instead, it referred the matter to the Bombay Chamber of Commerce and the Bombay Cotton Association for appropriate action to suppress the evil with the assistance and cooperation of the Bombay government.[60] The Bombay merchants remained adamant in their opposition to any legislative action. The Bombay Chamber of Commerce candidly explained its reason: as long as demand existed in Europe for inferior brands of cotton merchants would buy it, middlemen would mix it, and cultivators would grow it. This was the natural course of trade that legislation would not check.[61]

[57]Government of India to Secretary of State, Letter no. 21 (Judicial), 5 July 1881.

[58]Secretary of State to Viceroy, telegram, 30 Aug. 1881; Secretary of State to Government of Bombay, Despatch no. 31 (Revenue), 31 Aug. 1881; India, Revenue and Agriculture (Fibres and Silk) Proceedings, November 1881, nos. 1–7.

[59]Bombay, Rev. Dept. Comp., XLVII (1891), no. 814.

[60]*Proceedings of the Manchester Chamber of Commerce*, 29 July, 24 Sept., and 29 Oct. 1884.

[61]Bombay Chamber of Commerce to Government of Bombay, 15 Jan. 1885. Bombay, Rev. Dept. Comp., LXXVII (1885), no. 18.

The Bombay government, no doubt unwilling to get its fingers burned, declined to take any action. Not surprisingly, adulteration continued. More than a quarter of a century later, protests were still being made about the bad quality of Indian cotton. Thus in 1912 the International Federation of Master Spinners' and Manufacturers' Associations pressed for legislative action to prevent the adulteration of Indian cotton. The evils complained of were precisely those that had existed before the American Civil War and that had prompted the enactment of special legislation in 1863: cotton was being watered in ginning and pressing factories in order to increase its weight; saltpetre and cotton seed were being pressed into the bales for the same reason; and different varieties were being mixed before ginning and the mixture sold as a superior variety.[62] In 1919, the Indian Cotton Committee, which had been appointed by the Government of India to inquire into the possibility of extending the growth of long-stapled cotton in India, reported that adulteration of Indian cotton had "made it a by-word in certain markets almost throughout the history of the British connexion with India."[63] But even at this late date it could not recommend re-enactment of the cotton-frauds legislation because of the continuing hostility of mercantile opinion.[64]

In the conflict over cotton frauds legislation in mid-nineteenth century India, there were four main contestants whose positions shifted at different stages of the battle: the Bombay merchants, the Lancashire manufacturers, the Government of India, and the Bombay government. The British Government played the role of final arbiter.

Why did the Bombay merchants come to oppose so vehemently legislation which had originally been passed at the behest of the Bombay Chamber of Commerce? They had two practical objections: the inspection establishment and the export fee. But their opposition went deeper. In the early part of the American Civil War, an important section of the Bombay Chamber of Commerce believed that Indian cotton could retain a major share of the British market if its quality could be improved. For this reason they were able to secure passage of the legislation with relatively little commercial opposition. But by 1870 American cotton had recaptured the dominant position in the English market that it had enjoyed before 1861, and support for cotton frauds legislation withered. At the same time new markets were gained in continental Europe which provided a steady demand for cheap, short-stapled Indian cotton for which its spinning machinery was specially constructed. No complaints came from European importers about the quality of Indian cotton and this seemed to

[62]Arno Schmidt, *Cotton Growing in India* (Manchester: International Federation of Master Cotton Spinners' and Manufacturers' Associations, Reports, 1912), p. 82.
[63]*Report of the Indian Cotton Committee* (Calcutta, 1919), p. 175.
[64]Cotton frauds legislation was finally re-enacted in Bombay in 1936.

the merchants of Bombay additional evidence that special legislation was no longer needed. In addition, among Indian merchants in Bombay there was a distinct feeling that the legislation was discriminatory, in that it was really directed at them rather than at their European colleagues. They also argued that there was no reciprocal legislation protecting them from abuses committed by Lancashire manufacturers and exporters of piece goods.

The same factors determined the attitude of the Lancashire manufacturers. In Manchester as in Bombay there were those who hoped that India might become a permanent alternative to America as a source of raw cotton. This belief was strongly held by the Cotton Supply Association. But the readiness with which Lancashire manufacturers turned once more to America after the Civil War was over belied these hopes and in 1872 the Cotton Supply Association was disbanded. Support in Lancashire for the Cotton Frauds Act disappeared with it. Moreover, British manufacturers developed a further reason for wanting the Act repealed. In the 1870s they began to feel the competition of the Indian mill industry. They began a vigorous campaign for the removal of any legislative advantages enjoyed by Indian manufacturers. Chief among these were the cotton import duties, but the export fee was also seen as conferring some benefit on the Indian industry which was not shared by Lancashire. The fee was levied under the terms of the Cotton Frauds Act; it followed that the act must be repealed.

In pressing for repeal, the mercantile interests in both Bombay and Manchester, organized through their Chambers of Commerce, received increasing support from the Government of India. Opposition from that quarter was grounded in economic theory. Cotton frauds legislation represented state interference in private trade and was unacceptable to men of free trade views, such as Northbrook, Lytton, Hume, Strachey, and Stephen. The Bombay government, on the other hand, changed from opposition to legislation to regulate the cotton trade, to reluctant acquiescence because of the exceptional circumstances created by the American war, and finally to wholehearted support. This conversion was due both to the effectiveness of the Act in stopping the worst forms of adulteration, and to the government's desire to give a permanent stimulus to a new and better quality export staple. It always stressed the deterrent rather than the punitive aspects of the law which it did not see as being designed to prevent trade in inferior cotton but only to prevent any disguise of the real quality of such cotton.

The Bombay government weakened its case for maintaining the legislation in two ways. It failed to give detailed and workable regulations to guide the officers appointed to enforce the Act when it was first passed. Lack of such regulations contributed to the image of inefficiency which the cotton frauds department acquired during the early years of its existence. Second, a major weakness of the Act was its loose definition of the term "adulteration"; inspectors sometimes construed it in a way which proved harassing to trade. These two defects are explained by the reluctance with which the Bombay government agreed to the legislation in 1863 and to its well-meaning desire not to disturb the course of trade unduly. By the time it had been converted to support of the legislation the climate of commercial opinion had changed. The Bombay government then had to defend its case for state intervention against arguments drawn from the prevailing principles of *laissez-faire*, and expressed by powerful and well-organized commercial groups. Thus the Cotton Frauds Act was destroyed by the ideology of the age and the organized self-interest of its opponents. With it collapsed India's first attempt to use the power of the state to regulate the course of trade. With it also collapsed another attempt by the state to embark on a program of agricultural development. Meanwhile, another clear demonstration had been given of the way in which British rule was open to the charge of subserving Indian to British interests in matters of economic policy. This charge, reinforced by Lancashire's success in securing abolition of the cotton duties, was to become an important element in nationalist propaganda against British rule in the closing years of the nineteenth century.

7

CONCLUSION

THE CLASSICAL VIEW of nineteenth century British imperialism claims interest in empire to be at low ebb in the middle decades of the century and at full tide after 1880. According to this view, the free trade ideology of the Manchester School was responsible for mid-century indifference. Explanations for the subsequent rise of the "new imperialism" vary: they include the surplus capital theory of Hobson and Lenin; the theory of increasing competition among the great powers for markets and raw materials; the theory that imperialism was merely the overseas extension of diplomatic rivalries and nationalistic competition originating in Europe; and the theory that colonies were necessary as outlets for surplus population.[1] But all agree in contending that late-Victorian imperialism represented a sharp change from the indifference of the mid-century, and that this change was due to the decline of free trade beliefs.[2]

[1] Cf. M.E. Chamberlain, *The New Imperialism* (London: Historical Association, 1970), pp. 22ff.

[2] This classical view may be in part a function of a particular image of empire: one that sees it in the mid-nineteenth century in terms of the white colonies of settlement and in the late century in terms of the scramble for Africa. In neither period is sufficient attention paid to India. This image, in turn, is partly a function of the geographical and historical world view which sees Africa as a "continent" and India as a "country." On this see Marshall G. S. Hodgson, "The Interrelations of Societies in History," *Comparative Studies in Society and History*, II (1963), pp. 227–250.

The evidence of British policy in India in the mid-nineteenth century casts doubt on the classical view. In this period, the Indian economy appeared to the Lancashire cotton interests as an ideal complement to Great Britain's economy: India would provide both raw materials for British industry and a vast market for British manufactures. Commercial penetration of India required a planned program of public works and significant investment by the state. Political control of India made possible both the annexation of new territories, thus widening the area of commercial penetration, and the application of an economic philosophy – free trade – which would ensure unrestricted opportunities for the British export trade. Throughout the so-called era of indifference, the cotton interests of Lancashire called for a program of internal Indian development to facilitate accelerated British commercial penetration, and for a tariff policy which would integrate the Indian economy into Great Britain's by providing free access for British manufactured goods.

The specific examples given in this book show how British free trade doctrines and British imperial interests were juxtaposed and harmonized in the mid-nineteenth century. In its attitude to the tariff, Lancashire showed most clearly the imperialism inherent in free trade attitudes in the mid-Victorian period. British statesmen responsible for the governance of India, whether Liberal or Conservative, were careful to pay attention to the demands of the Lancashire cotton lobby in determining Indian tariff policy. Canning, Elgin, and Laing in India, and Wood, Salisbury, and Cranbrook in England were equally sensitive to the political necessity of an Indian tariff that accorded with the general belief of the merchants that Indian duties on imported British cotton manufactures threatened the whole economic basis of the Lancashire cotton industry.[3]

If the statesmen differed at all with the merchants on this issue, it was only over the question of timing, not of principle. Cobden himself reached the heart of the matter when he commented that "if you talk to our Lancashire friends they argue that unless we occupied India there would be no trade with that country, or that someone else would monopolize it, forgetting that this is the old protectionist theory which they formerly used to ridicule."[4] Both Laing in the Legislative Council of India in 1862, when he argued that Indian fiscal policy must not hurt British trade interests, and Jacob Bright in the House of Commons in 1875, when he complained of the "unfairness" of India's advantage in the manufacture of cloth and yarn, showed the so-called free traders' concern with protecting the Indian market for British exports. And in securing first the reduction of

[3]Arthur Redford, *Manchester Merchants and Foreign Trade,* 2 vols. (Manchester: Manchester University Press, 1934 and 1956), II, p. 26.

[4]Quoted by William D. Grampp, *The Manchester School of Economics* (Stanford: Stanford University Press, 1960), p. 125.

the Indian cotton duties and later their abolition, Lancashire demonstrated the way in which British economic imperialism in the mid-nineteenth century involved the exploitation of political dominion for continuing material advantage.[5]

The effort to develop India as a major source of raw cotton provides an additional example of the ways in which the arts of political manipulation gave aid to the craft of enterprise in the mid-Victorian era. In 1863, John Cheetham, the president of the Cotton Supply Association, asked the Manchester Chamber of Commerce what use India was to Great Britain if she could not be made into a great competitor with America as a source of raw material for Lancashire's mills. He called on the government to use whatever means were necessary to achieve this end and declared that he hoped for something better than "the usual stale answer, namely, that it was contrary to the rules of political economy."[6] Using its well-tried political techniques, Lancashire was able to force the Government of India to retreat from its stand, which was fully supported by Sir Charles Wood, that it should not intervene in the question of cotton supply. Wood firmly believed that the operation of the law of supply and demand alone would produce the results desired by the cotton interests and that increased cultivation of cotton in India was simply a question of price. As long as he remained Secretary of State, the measures taken by the government to improve the supply of cotton to Britain were restrained. But after his resignation in 1866 they expanded into a large-scale cotton improvement program, involving the experimental cultivation of cotton, the establishment of model farms, and the first use of legislative power in India in the fields of production, marketing, and trade, in an effort to improve the quality of Indian cotton.

In its demand for a public works program that would improve communications in India, to facilitate both the export of raw cotton and the import of manufactured goods, Lancashire again departed from the orthodox principles of *laissez-faire*. In this field, there was no conflict between the government authorities and the Lancashire manufacturers. Men like Sir Charles Wood agreed with the Manchester School that the

[5]Manchester's interest in Africa as a market for textiles in the late nineteenth century and its pressure on the British government for action were qualitatively no different from its mid-nineteenth century attitude to the Indian tariff. It merely illustrates the continuity in British imperial policy. Similarly, the British used the device of the Chartered Company to open up areas of Africa, as the East India Company had been used to expand British influence in India. The British also extended to Africa the device of indirect rule used in India after 1857, when a large part of the sub-continent remained under the control of native princes.

[6]Quoted by Oliver MacDonagh, 'The Anti-Imperialism of Free Trade," *Economic History Review* 2nd series, XIV (1961–62), p. 496. The desire to escape dependence on foreign countries for supplies of raw materials was, of course, a central feature of both seventeenth-century mercantilism and of modern imperialism.

government had a positive duty to develop India's communications. This belief was best illustrated by the costly guarantee system of building railways – "private enterprise at public risk" as it has aptly been called.[7] But it was also illustrated by the road, port, and canal schemes that were hastily conceived and implemented, without regard to cost, to satisfy Lancashire's persistent demand for government action to improve communications in India.

Taken together all these policies show Lancashire's awareness of the great importance of India to British trade in the mid-nineteenth century. In pursuit of its interests, the principles of *laissez-faire* proved no handicap to the Manchester School. Indeed, the apparent paradox of the demand of Lancashire free traders for extensive government intervention to ensure free access to the Indian market for British manufactured goods, for the development of India as a source of raw cotton, and for the underwriting of railway construction on a grand scale, lends further support to the argument of J. B. Brebner that *laissez-faire* in mid-nineteenth century England was essentially a myth – a slogan which covered the demand of the industrial entrepreneurs not only for new freedoms but also for new services.[8] The age of free trade was indeed an era of imperialism, measured by the standard of British policy in India. The hardheaded men of Lancashire did not find it inconsistent to cut the cloth of economic theory to suit their practical interests.

[7]Daniel Thorner, *Investment in Empire: British Railway and Steam Shipping Enterprise in India, 1825–1849* (Philadelphia: University of Pennsylvania Press, 1950), uses the phrase as the title of ch. 7.

[8]J. Bartlett Brebner, "Laissez Faire and State Intervention in Nineteenth-Century Britain," *Journal of Economic History, Supplement*, VIII (1948), pp. 59–73; Thorner, *Investment in Empire*, pp. 178–79.

BIBLIOGRAPHY

A. UNPUBLISHED SOURCES

I. PRIVATE PAPERS

1. Foreign and Commonwealth Office – India Office Library, London

   a. Halifax Collection, MSS. Eur. F. 78

   This collection contains the India correspondence of Sir Charles Wood, first Earl of Halifax, as President of the Board of Control for the East India Company, 1853–55 and Secretary of State for India, 1859–66. It consists of twenty-nine volumes of letter books, which are manuscript copies of letters Wood wrote to officials in India as well as correspondence on Indian affairs with persons in England; and original copies of letters received by Wood from officials in India and persons in England on Indian matters. Since Wood was the minister in charge of Indian affairs at a time when such issues as the tariff, cotton supply, and public works were of critical importance, this collection is of crucial interest in determining British attitudes to India in the mid-nineteenth century.

   b. Elgin Papers, MSS. Eur. F. 83

   Elgin's term as Viceroy and Governor-General of India covered the period from March 1862 to November 1863 and was cut short by his untimely death. The six volumes of his letters to the Secretary of State and the two portfolios of letters from the Secretary of State are duplicated in the Halifax Collection, except that the latter include enclosures to Wood's letters. There are also sixteen volumes of Elgin's private correspondence with officials in India as well as miscellaneous papers. The collection has been comprehensively catalogued by M. C. Mountfort (Mrs. M. C. Poulter).

c.   Richard Temple Papers, MSS. Eur. F. 86

d.   John Lawrence Papers, MSS. Eur. F. 90
The papers of Sir John Lawrence as Viceroy and Governor-General of India from 1864–69 include thirty-nine volumes of his correspondence with four Secretaries of State (Wood, de Grey, Cranborne, and Northcote) and with numerous correspondents in India.

e.   Lytton Papers, MSS. Eur. E. 218
The six volumes of correspondence with the Secretary of State (series 516) and nine volumes of letters from persons in England (series 517) were consulted.

2. Leeds Public Library

Canning Papers
This collection was read at the estate record office of the Earl of Harewood, Harewood House, Leeds. Eighty bound volumes of Canning's correspondence with the Presidents of the Board of Control and Secretaries of State for India, and with officials in India, were consulted. There are registers and indexes for these volumes. There is also some correspondence with Lancashire people in the Private Secretary's correspondence, for which there are also registers and indexes.

3. Manchester Central Reference Library

Proceedings of the Manchester Chamber of Commerce
Volumes 5 to 8, covering the years 1849–79, were consulted.

II. Official Records

1. Foreign and Commonwealth Office – India Office Records, London

It is unnecessary to list the hundreds of volumes of despatches to India, Madras, and Bombay; letters from India, Madras, and Bombay; the Home correspondence; and the proceedings of the various departments of the Governments of India, Madras, and Bombay. The relevant volumes of the Legislative, Public, Public. Works, Revenue, and Separate Revenue despatches to India, Madras, and Bombay have been read, as well as the collections to them, and the corresponding series of letters from India, Madras, and Bombay. The Home correspondence was of particular importance to this study since it includes a large number of letters received from various groups in Lancashire, notably the Manchester Chamber of Commerce and the Cotton Supply Association, and the Secretary of State's replies to them. The proceedings of the Governments of India, Madras, and Bombay have also been read, as well as the annual administration reports of the various provinces, for the period covered by this study. All these documents are listed in the India Office Library's *List of General Records, 1599–1879*.

2. National Archives of India, New Delhi

The proceedings of the Government of India in the various departments were consulted. They are more complete than the bound and printed volumes contained in the India Office Library and include notes by the Governor-General and members of his Council which were not sent to London, but were kept with the original documents. These "keep-with" notes, as they were called, often give revealing insights into the reactions of the Government of India to policy directives received in despatches from the Secretary of State.

3. Maharashtra State Records Office, Bombay

The Revenue Department Compilations of the Government of Bombay were consulted. The compilations were bound annually in alphabetical order of their main subjects. They are more complete than the Bombay Revenue Proceedings found in the India Office Library and include the rough notes of the secretary in charge of the department, the rough minutes of the member of the Governor's Council responsible for the department, and notations by the Governor himself. The annual administration reports of the Bombay Cotton Department were also consulted.

B. OFFICIAL PRINTED SOURCES

I. PARLIAMENTARY PAPERS

The following references indicate the session, volume number, and number of the paper.

1847   XLII (439). Cotton: Measures taken since 1836 to promote the cultivation.
1847–48   IX (511). Growth of Cotton in India: Report from the Select Committee, with Minutes of Evidence, Appendix, and Index.
1857–58   XIV (416). Railways (Delay in Construction): Report from the Select Committee, with Proceedings, Minutes of Evidence and Appendix.
XLII (210-VII). Railways: Extent of, with an account of the progress made and expense incurred.
1859   XXIII (81). Indian Tariff: Correspondence.
1860   LII (54). Navigation and Irrigation Works of the Godavery River: Letters from Captain Haig, and Minute by Sir Charles Trevelyan.
LII (2669). Report on Railways to the End of 1859.
1862   XL (55). Godavery River: Minutes, &c. relating to the opening up of the river to Berar, from 1st January 1860; and Reports and Correspondence of the Engineers and others employed.
LV (88). Cotton: Return of the Cotton Goods exported to the British East Indies, and the Cotton imported therefrom, 1855 to 1861.
1863   XLIII (81). Sedasheghur Harbour: Correspondence.
XLIII (307). Sedasheghur: Correspondence relative to the Harbour and Roads thereto.
XLIV (132). Cultivation of Cotton in India: Correspondence, 1860–63.
XLIV (132. I). Cultivation of Cotton in India: Further Return.
1864   XLII (248). Opening up of the River Godavery: Minutes, Reports, and Correspondence of the Engineers and others employed.
XLII (99). Sedasheghur (Carwar) Harbour and Roads Leading thereto: Further Correspondence.
1865   XL (345). Financial Measures for India in 1865–66, and Provision of Funds for Public Works: Letter from the Government of India, dated 6th January 1865, &c. Correspondence regarding the Income Tax.

1867   LXXII (C. 3817). Statistical Abstract relating to British India, from 1840 to 1865.

L (148). Revision of Tariff Valuations.

1867–68 L (201). Opening up of the River Godavery: Minutes and Correspondence of the Secretary of State, the Governor-General, &c., and Reports and Correspondence of the Engineers and others employed.

1868–69 XLVI (397). Cotton: Report by Mr. H. Rivett-Carnac, Cotton Commissioner for the Central Provinces and Berar, for the year 1867.

1871   L (55). Cotton: Reports from Mr. H. Rivett-Carnac, Cotton Commissioner for the Central Provinces and Berar, for the year 1868–69.

1872   VIII (327). East India Finance: Report from the Select Committee with Proceedings.

1873   XII (354). East India Finance: Third Report from the Select Committee, with Proceedings, Minutes of Evidence regarding Local Taxation and its relation to Imperial Taxation, Military Expenditures, and General Finances, Appendix, and Index.

LXIX (C. 870). Statistical Abstract relating to British India from 1863 to 1872.

1876   LVI (56). Indian Tariff Act, 1875: Correspondence.

LVI (70). Indian Tariff Act, 1875: Dissent by Member of the Council of India upon Despatch of 11th November 1875.

LVI (219). Tariff: Financial Despatch No. 354, of 15th July 1875.

LVI (333). Tariff Act, 1875: Dissents and Minutes by Members of the Council of India on Despatches of the Secretary of State, dated 31st May 1875.

LVI (C. 1515). Indian Tariff Act of 1875: Further correspondence.

1877   LXXXV (C. 1840). Statistical Abstract relating to British India, from 1866–67 to 1875–76.

1878–79 IX (312). Report from the Select Committee on East India (Public Works).

LV (165). Financial Statement of the Government of India for 1879–80, with Appendix of Correspondence regarding the appointment of a commission to inquire into certain questions affecting the Customs Tariff (Indian Tariff Act, 1875) and their Report.

LV (188). Duties on Cotton Goods: Dissents recorded by Members of the Council of the Governor-General of India.

LV (240). Council of India and Cotton Duties.

LV (241). Articles in the Tariff of India: Further Papers including Report of a Commission.

LV (392). Cotton Duties.

1909   LXIV (89). Annual Lists and General Index of the Parliamentary Papers relating to the East Indies published during the years 1801 to 1907 inclusive.

II. OTHER OFFICIAL PUBLICATIONS

Great Britain, *Parliamentary Debates*, 3rd series, 1860–80.

India, *Legislative Council Proceedings*, vols. 1–7 (1854–61); new series, vols. I-XXI (1862–82).

Bombay, *Legislative Council Proceedings*, vols. I-XXI (1862–82).

Report of the Indian Cotton Committee (Calcutta, 1919).

C. NEWSPAPER

Cotton Supply Reporter, Manchester, 1858–1872.

D. CONTEMPORARY WORKS

A.F.B., *Statistical Tables Relating to Indian Cotton* (Bombay, 1889).

Arnold, R. A., *The History of the Cotton Famine* (London: Saunders, Otley, 1864).

Cassels, Walter R., *Cotton: An Account of its Culture in Bombay Presidency* (Bombay, 1862).

Denison, Sir William, *Varieties of Viceregal Life*, 2 vols. (London: Longmans, Green, 1870).

Ellison, Thomas, *The Cotton Trade of Great Britain* (London: Effingham Wilson, 1886; reprinted by Frank Cass, 1968).

Haig, C. A., *Memories of the Life of General F. T. Haig by his Wife* (London; Marshall Bros., 1902).

Haig, F. T., *Report on the Navigability of the River Godavari and some of its Affluents*, 2 pts. (Madras, 1856).

Haywood, G. R., *India as a Source of the Supply of Cotton* (Manchester, 1862).

Mackay, Alexander, *Western India* (London: N. Cooke, 1853).

Moore, A. T., *Indian Cotton, Its Adulteration and Acts Passed to Suppress the Same* (Bombay, 1872).

Smith, Samuel, *The Cotton Trade of India* (London, 1863).

Temple, Sir Richard, *Men and Events of My Time in India* (London: John Murray, 1882).

Walton, W., *A Short History of Cotton, its Culture, Trade and Manufacture in the Belgaum and Kaladgi Districts of the Bombay Presidency* (Bombay, 1880).

Watson, John Forbes, *Report on Cotton Gins and on the Cleaning and Quality of Indian Cotton*, 2 vols. (London, 1879).

Watts, Isaac, *The Cotton Supply Association: Its Origins and Progress* (Manchester, 1871).

Watts, John, *The Facts of the Cotton Famine* (London, 1866; reprinted by Frank Cass, 1968).

E. BOOKS

Bearce, George D., *British Attitudes Towards India, 1784–1858* (London: Oxford University Press, 1961).

Bodelsen, C. A., *Studies in Mid-Victorian Imperialism* (Copenhagen: Glydendal, 1924).

Buckle, George Earle, *see* Monypenny, William Flavelle.

Cell, John W., *British Colonial Administration in the Mid-Nineteenth Century: The Policy-Making Process* (New Haven: Yale University Press, 1970).

Chamberlain, M. E., *The New Imperialism* (London: Historical Association, 1970).

Dyck, Harvey L., and Krosby, H. Peter (eds.), *Empire and Nations: Essays in Honour of Frederick H. Soward* (Toronto: University of Toronto Press, 1969).

Gopal, S., *British Policy in India, 1858–1905* (Cambridge: Cambridge University Press, 1965).

Grampp, William D., *The Manchester School of Economics* (Stanford: Stanford University Press, 1960).

Henderson, W. O., *The Lancashire Cotton Famine* (Manchester: Manchester University Press, 1934).

Hobson, J. A., *Imperialism: A Study*, 3rd edition (London: G. Allen and Unwin, 1938).

Jenks, Leland H., *The Migration of British Capital to 1875* (New York: Alfred Knopf, 1927).

Langer, W. L., *The Diplomacy of Imperialism, 1890–1902*, 2nd edition (New York: Alfred Knopf, 1951).

Lenin, V. I., *Selected Works: Two-Volume Edition* (Moscow, 1947).
Maccoby, S., *English Radicalism, 1853–1886* (London: Allen and Unwin, 1938).
Monypenny, William Flavelle, *The Life of Benjamin Disraeli, Earl of Beaconsfield*, 6 vols. Vol. III by W. F. Monypenny and G. E. Buckle; Vols. IV–VI by G. E. Buckle (London: John Murray, 1910–20).
Moore, R. J., *Sir Charles Wood's Indian Policy, 1853–66* (Manchester: Manchester University Press, 1966).
Moulton, E. C., *Lord Northbrook's Indian Administration* (Bombay: Asia Publishing House, 1968).
Platt, D. C. M., *Finance, Trade, and Politics: British Foreign Policy, 1815–1914* (Oxford: Clarendon Press, 1968).
Redford, Arthur, *Manchester Merchants and Foreign Trade*, 2 vols. (Manchester: Manchester University Press, 1934 and 1956).
Schmidt, Arno, *Cotton Growing in India* (Manchester: International Federation of Master Cotton Spinners' and Manufacturers Associations, Reports, 1912).
Schuyler, R. L., *The Fall of the Old Colonial System* (New York: Oxford University Press, 1945).
Silver, Arthur W., *Manchester Men and Indian Cotton, 1847–1872* (Manchester: Manchester University Press, 1966).
Thorner, Daniel, *Investment in Empire: British Railway and Steam Shipping Enterprise in India, 1825–1849* (Philadelphia: University of Pennsylvania Press, 1950).
Thornton, A. P., *Doctrines of Imperialism* (New York: Wiley, 1965).

F. ARTICLES

Brady, Eugene A., "A Reconsideration of the Lancashire 'Cotton Famine'," *Agricultural History*, XXXVII (1963), pp. 156–62.
Brebner, J. Bartlett, "Laissez Faire and State Intervention in Nineteenth-Century Britain," *Journal of Economic History, Supplement*, VIII (1948), pp. 59–73.
Creighton, D. G., "The Victorians and the Empire," *Canadian Historical Review*, XIX (1938), pp. 138–53.
Fieldhouse, David, "British Imperialism in the Late Eighteenth Century: Defence of Opulence?" in Kenneth Robinson and Frederick Madden (eds.), *Essays in Imperial Government Presented to Margery Perham* (Oxford: Basil Blackwell, 1963).
Furber, Holden, "The Theme of Imperialism and Colonialism in Modern Historical Writing on India," in C. H. Philips (ed.), *Historians of India, Pakistan and Ceylon* (London: Oxford University Press, 1961), pp. 332–43.
Gallagher, John, and Robinson Ronald, "The Imperialism of Free Trade," *Economic History Review*, 2nd series, VI (1953), pp. 1–15.
Gujral, Lalit, "Sir Louis Mallet's Mission to Lord Northbrook on the Question of the Cotton Duties," *Journal of Indian History*, XXXIX (1961), pp. 473–87.
Habakkuk, H. J., "Free Trade and Commercial Expansion, 1853–1870," *Cambridge History of the British Empire*, II (1940), pp. 751–805.
Harnetty, Peter, "Cotton Exports and Indian Agriculture, 1861–1870," *Economic History Review*, 2nd ser., XXIV (1971), pp. 414–29.
——, "The Cotton Improvement Program in India, 1865–1875," *Agricultural History*, XLIV (1970), pp. 379–92.
——, "Imperialism and Free Trade: Lancashire and India in the 1860s," in Harvey L. Dyck and H. Peter Krosby (eds.), *Empire and Nations: Essays in Honour of Frederick H. Soward* (Toronto: University of Toronto Press, 1969), pp. 163–179.

Harnetty, Peter, "The Imperialism of Free Trade: Lancashire, India, and The Cotton Supply Question, 1861–1865," *Journal of British Studies*, VI (1966), pp. 70–96.

——, "The Imperialism of Free Trade: Lancashire and the Indian Cotton Duties, 1859–1862," *Economic History Review*, 2nd ser., XVIII (1965), pp. 333–49.

——, "India and British Commercial Enterprise: The Case of the Manchester Cotton Company, 1860–64," *Indian Economic and Social History Review*, III (1966), pp. 396–421.

——, "The Indian Cotton Duties Controversy, 1894–1896," *English Historical Review*, LXXVII (1962), pp. 684–702.

——, " 'India's Mississippi': The River Godavari Navigation Scheme," *Journal of Indian History*, XLIII (1965), pp. 699–732.

Hodgson, Marshall G. S., "The Interrelations of Societies in History," *Comparative Studies in Society and History*, II (1963), pp. 227–50.

Landes, David S., "Some Thoughts on the Nature of Economic Imperialism," *Journal of Economic History*, XXI (1961), pp. 496–512.

Leacock, Seth, and Mandelbaum, David G., "A Nineteenth Century Development Project in India: The Cotton Improvement Program," *Economic Development and Cultural Change*, III (1955), pp. 334–41.

Logan, Frenise A., "The American Civil War: An Incentive to Western India's Experiments with Foreign Cotton Seeds?" *Agricultural History*, XXIX (1955), pp. 33–39.

——, "India's Loss of the British Cotton Market after 1865," *Journal of Southern History*, XXXI (1965), pp. 40–50.

MacDonagh, Oliver, "The Anti-Imperialism of Free Trade," *Economic History Review*, 2nd ser., XIV (1961–62), pp. 489–501.

MacPherson, W. J., "Investment in Indian Railways, 1845–1875," *Economic History Review*, 2nd ser., VIII (1955), pp. 177–86.

Mathew, W. M., "The Imperialism of Free Trade: Peru, 1820–70," *Economic History Review*, 2nd ser., XXI (1968), pp. 562–79.

Mehta, D. N., "Cotton Breeding in the Central Provinces and Berar," Indian Central Cotton Committee, *First Conference of Scientific Research Workers on Cotton in India* (Bombay, 1938), pp. 401–9.

Moore, R. J., "Imperialism and 'Free Trade' Policy in India, 1853–4," *Economic History Review*, 2nd ser., XVII (1964), pp. 135–45.

Platt, D. C. M., "The Imperialism of Free Trade: Some Reservations," *Economic History Review*, 2nd ser., XXI (1968), pp. 296–306.

Stembridge, Stanley R., "Disraeli and the Millstones," *Journal of British Studies*, V (1965–66), pp. 122–39.

Tripathi, Amales, "Manchester, India Office and the Tariff Controversy, 1858–1882," Indian Historical Records Commission, *Proceedings*, XXXVI, Part 2 (1961), pp. 13–19.

——, Dwijendra, "Opportunism of Free Trade – The Sedasheogarh Harbour Project, 1855–1865," *Indian Economic and Social History Review*, V (1968), pp. 389–405.

Williamson, J.A., "Phases of Empire History," *History*, XXXIII (1948), pp. 49–71.

INDEX

Aberdeen, Lord, 60
American Civil War: and cotton supply
  question, 22, 38–39, 42–44, 46–49, 62,
  75, 83, 105; effect on cotton prices, 31,
  46, 86, 88, 89, 102; impact on cotton
  cultivation in India, 38–40, 45–46,
  52–54, 83, 89, 98; effect on public
  works policy in India, 62–69; stimulus
  to Godavari navigation scheme, 77;
  and cotton frauds legislation, 102–3
American planters, 83, 84, 85
Amraoti cotton, 90
Argyll, Duke of, 55, 76–77
Ashburner, Lionel, 89–91, 94, 95 *n*. 35
Association of Bleachers and Dyers, 15–
  16, 19

Baring, Evelyn, 34
Bazley, Thomas, 6, 14, 17, 37
Bengal Chamber of Commerce, 12–13,
  107–8
Berar, 4, 69, 72–73, 89–90, 91, 106, 116.
  See also Central Provinces
Bernard, C. E., 116
Birley, Hugh, 33, 115 *n*. 46
Blackburn, 16
Board of Trade, 16
Bombay Association, 110

Bombay Chamber of Commerce, 91,
  102–12, 119–21
Bombay presidency: tariff valuations in,
  12, 13 *n*. 16, 14; cotton commissioner
  for, 49–52, 85–92, 94–96, 99; alleged
  famine conditions in, 53; road building
  in, 65. *See also* Cotton Frauds Act;
  Dharwar American cotton; Dharwar-
  Karwar road; Karwar port scheme;
  Khandesh
Brice, A. C., 42
Bright, Jacob, 33, 115 *n*. 46, 124
Bright, John: on cotton supply question,
  36–37, 48, 59–60; opposition to renewal
  of East India Company charter, 38,
  60; and Godavari navigation scheme,
  71
British imperial interests. *See* Great
  Britain, imperial interests

Campbell, A. H., 109
Canada, 2, 3, 80
Canning, Lord: anticipation of budget
  deficit, 8; and Indian import duties,
  9–10, 19–21, 124; interview with
  Manchester Chamber of Commerce,
  38; on cotton supply question, 41–42
Cassels, Walter, 44, 102 *n*. 3

134